BRITAIN'S ROAD TUNNELS

MARK CHATTERTON

AMBERLEY

This book is dedicated to the memory of my father, William Paul Chatterton, who first took me through the Mersey Tunnel all those years ago.

First published 2020

Amberley Publishing
The Hill, Stroud,
Gloucestershire, GL5 4EP

www.amberley-books.com

ISBN: 978 1 3981 0028 2 (print)
ISBN: 978 1 3981 0029 9 (ebook)

British Library Cataloguing in Publication Data.
A catalogue record for this book is available from the British Library.

Typeset in 10pt on 13pt Celeste.
Origination by Amberley Publishing.
Printed in the UK.

Contents

Introduction

Tunnels come in all shapes and sizes and are found in most countries all over the world. They have a useful part to play in moving goods from A to B; saving a much longer journey if the tunnel wasn't there. Not only do roads and railways use tunnels, canals, rivers, electrical cables and even sewers all benefit from their construction too. There is something quite magical about travelling through a tunnel, leaving one place behind, only to resurface minutes later in a completely different place.

My introduction to the world of road tunnels began at a very early age, when I was a toddler in the 1950s. I can distinctly remember my father taking me in his car through the Mersey Tunnel as it was then known. At the time we lived in the Mossley Hill district of Liverpool, where I was born, and we would often go over to the Wirral to visit my grandparents who lived in Ellesmere Port. Going through the tunnel was the easiest route to take, as the alternative was to drive to Widnes and take the old Transporter bridge across the Mersey to Runcorn in Cheshire, a very long-winded journey and much longer time wise. The main attraction of the tunnel for me was not all the bright lights and the bends; nor was it knowing that you had reached the bottom of the tunnel and now it was uphill all the way to the exit. No, the attraction for me and for many people was coming out at the other end into a completely different world from the one we had left several minutes ago.

This fascination with tunnels has never left me and I have always found travelling through a road tunnel an interesting experience. So this book comes not just out of a love of road tunnels, but also a desire to find out more about them; such as how they were built, why they were built and who were the people who designed, engineered and constructed them. In fact, for the past ten years whenever I have been away from home, partly with my work and partly on holiday, I have looked out for road tunnels in many areas, photographing them and learning about them.

It has been an interesting journey, discovering new tunnels in the most unlikely places. For whatever reason, the majority of road tunnels are found in the South East of England. London, as you would expect, has by far the most road tunnels per square mile. In fact, there are no fewer than twenty road tunnels within a 10-mile radius of Tower Bridge. Kent is the county with the most road tunnels, having eleven according to my calculations.

The big question many of you will be asking is, 'What actually is a road tunnel?' This is a difficult question to answer exactly, as there are various definitions out there which can confuse the issue. Let's start with the word 'tunnel'. At its very basic, a tunnel is a hole going into some earth which emerges at an exit. Going one stage further, we can say that a tunnel is a hole or tube which goes under a river or into some rocks and emerges at the other side of that particular obstacle. As to what constitutes a road tunnel, most people would say that it is a roadway which carries motor vehicles or road traffic through a tunnel. For this book I would define a road tunnel as one that has been built over a public road to carry motor vehicles, particularly cars, to travel under a hill, river, building or other obstacle.

Regarding its length, many people say a tunnel is an underground passage which is longer than it is wide. Yet some people say a tunnel is a roadway or railway line which when you enter it there is no light to be seen at the other end. Not all tunnels fit this definition of course. Certainly, there are different definitions from different authorities which can confuse the issue. In the UK, the Department for Transport defines a road tunnel as 'a subsurface highway structure enclosed for a length of 150 metres/164 yards or more'. That definition fits most of the major road tunnels in Great Britain such as the Dartford, Clyde and Tyne tunnels. In this book the principal tunnels in the first two chapters use the UK Department for Transport definition, but for the other chapters I have allowed shorter tunnels to be included, as long as they are noticeably longer than they are wide. So, it can be argued that there are many of these shorter road tunnels which go under buildings, railway lines and airport runways for example, which most people would agree are tunnels. I have included these as well, as I would argue that they are tunnels and not bridges, or under bridges, due to both their length and width, and the fact that they are covered or enclosed roadways, continuing for longer than they are wide.

Another question to take into consideration is that of underpasses, which I have also included in some cases. The definition of an underpass is also a difficult question. An underpass at its very basic is a roadway that passes under another road (or railway line). Yet if the road/railway line it passes under is longer than it is wide, it can be seen as a tunnel due to its length. Indeed, some underpasses are also known as tunnels, such as the Strand Underpass in London, which is also called the Kingsway Tunnel. Where an underpass is just too short to be 'tunnel like', I have not included it. For this reason, I have excluded such underpasses as the ones at Euston Road, Blackfriars and Croydon in London.

One of the difficulties in researching this book has been finding information on certain tunnels, especially the newer ones. Strangely, there seems to be more information on the older tunnels like the Blackwall and Mersey tunnels, as opposed to the newer ones like the Medway or the Roundhill tunnels. Finding accurate lengths of some tunnels has been hard. This has not been helped by different sources stating different lengths. For example, I found four different lengths given for the Meir Tunnel in Stoke-on-Trent. These were 248, 260, 280 and 284 metres! So just who do you believe? To the best of my knowledge all the information that I have provided in this book is correct at the time of publication, but I am sure the reader will accept that in some cases it has been impossible to be completely correct when it comes to the actual length of certain tunnels. For this reason, I have said that a tunnel 'is approximately...' to cover this variance. As to units used, I have in every case given the measurements in both imperial and metric.

To sum up, I have tried to include as much detail as possible on the majority of the tunnels covered in this book, such as its history, why it was built, the construction method used and its length. The Internet has been a great help in finding out more about a certain tunnel and I would recommend the website, instantstreetview.com, as well as YouTube for giving you the experience of 'travelling' through a tunnel, even if you can't physically be there. Hopefully you will discover tunnels that you never knew existed. I certainly did when researching this book, even as I was nearing the deadline! No doubt someone reading this book will know about a tunnel that has not been covered in this book. In that case you can let me know via my tunnels Facebook page – Road Tunnels of Great Britain – and I will try and include it in future editions of this book.

Mark Chatterton
Essex
November 2019

Acknowledgments

I would like to thank the following for their help in providing information and permission to use photographs for use in this book:

Bruce Chandler at Historic Environment Scotland; Clare at The Tunnel, Charmouth, Dorset; Megan Evans at the National Trust; Graham Pearce at the Road Tunnel Association; Mark Price at Leeds City Council, plus the taxi drivers who took me to various road tunnels in several British towns.

Thanks to the following people for providing their own photographs for use in this book: Sue Banham, Jim Chaucer, Nick Hartington, Allan Heron, Colin Shepperton, Graham Upwey, Ben Warmley.

Last but not least a big thank you to my wife, Wendy, who has assisted me by taking many of the photographs for this book.

All photographs by the author unless stated.

Glossary

There are several engineering terms regarding tunnels and their construction which I use quite regularly throughout the book. To help the reader understand the meanings of these words, I have included this glossary.

Bi-directional: where traffic on the roadway goes in both directions.

Bore: the name given to the inside part of a tunnel, or tube.

Bored: this is the name given to the type of tunnel construction where a tunnel is cut out of the rocks that it goes through. In the early days of tunnel construction tunnels were dug out with shovels and pickaxes, often with several men working together on a 'tunnel shield' (see below). As time has gone on tunnel construction has involved the use of a tunnel boring machine, or 'mole', which cuts into the rock using a number of circular blades built into a shield that chip away at the rock.

Crown: the name given to the highest part of the tunnel tube, which is the roof of the tunnel.

Cut-and-cover: another method of tunnel construction where a shallow trench is dug out first, the floor put in place and then covered over to create a tunnel. This is known as 'bottom up' cut-and-cover. The other version is called 'top down', where narrow trenches are cut and then filled in with concrete to create the walls. Then the roof part is added before the rest of the tunnel is dug out.

Immersed Tube: the method of tunnel construction where a tunnel is put into place under water. It involves the construction of a trench along a river or seabed, with a concrete tube being lowered into place into the trench at the bottom of the river or seabed. The remaining space in the trench is filled in and the tube is connected to other tubes at either end which take the tunnel back out to the surface.

Invert: this is the name given to the lowest part of the tunnel, usually the tunnel floor.

Nadir: the lowest point that is reached in a tunnel. Usually the halfway point where the tunnel reaches its deepest and then starts to climb up again to the surface.

New Austrian Method: this is a modern method of tunnel construction, which is used where the rock being dug out might be unstable. During the tunnel excavation, a layer of concrete is sprayed immediately onto the rock and bolts are put in place to strengthen the tube.

Pipe Jacking: another modern method of tunnel construction which is similar to boring, except that the machine used utilises hydraulic jacks to push pipes into the tunnel behind the machine to strengthen the rock around it.

Portal: the name given to the entrance or the open end of a tunnel.

Single carriageway: where the road in a tunnel is only wide enough for one vehicle to pass through at a time.

Tunnel Shield: a metal frame which is placed by the rock that is being cut out as the tunnel is being excavated.

Twin Bore: where a tunnel has two separate tubes or roadways, usually running parallel with each other.

CHAPTER 1

Road Tunnels on Major Trunk Roads

This section includes all the main road tunnels that can be found on the Major Trunk roads, including the Motorways and 'A' roads of Great Britain. They all have their dedicated name and, in most cases, they also have a road sign with the name of the tunnel on it.

Bell Common Tunnel, M25, Epping, Essex

The Bell Common Tunnel is situated to the west of Junction 27 of the M25 where it intersects with the M11. The tunnel is 560 yards/512 metres in length, and this is displayed along with its name on road signs at either end of the tunnel. It has two bores, each consisting of four lanes and a hard shoulder. Lying where it is, the Bell Common Tunnel is one of the busiest tunnels on the Trans European Road Network (TERN) with an average daily traffic count (AADT) of 140,000 vehicles a day. It is one of only two road tunnels on the M25 and is the only road tunnel which is completely in Essex. Construction on the tunnel started in 1982 and it was first opened to traffic in 1984. The tunnel was opened by the Transport Minister, Chris Mole, two months ahead of schedule, and a whole two years before the M25 was officially opened. Its name comes from Bell Common above it, which is situated to the south of the town of Epping. The tunnel was constructed using the cut-and-cover method and this meant that the cricket pitch above had to be cut up and then restored in order for the tunnel to be built. A tunnel was chosen, as opposed to a cutting, to minimise noise and disruption here with the town of Epping lying just to the north and Epping Forest being just to the south.

The tunnel was completely refurbished in the period October 2008 to March 2010 at a cost of £90 million. The refurbishment works included completely changing the ventilation system and renewing the electrical systems, in order to be compliant with new fire regulations. The tunnel was also extended by 44 yards/40 metres in order to cope with newly installed fans. The whole project won the Best Practise Award at the 2010 British Construction Awards. Then, in 2013, the carriageway within the tunnel was extended from three lanes to four as part of the M25 widening programme.

The eastern entrance to the Bell Common Tunnel on the M25. Note the length of tunnel sign in yards. (Wendy Chatterton)

Blackwall Tunnels, A102, Greenwich/Tower Hamlets, London

Situated in London's East End, this pair of road tunnels were opened approximately seventy years apart – in 1897 and 1967. They link Poplar and the A12 in the north with Greenwich and the A2 in the south. Before they were built the nearest road crossing of the River Thames was London Bridge, over 5 miles away. There was a demand for a crossing of the Thames here from both local residents and merchants who had to depend on unreliable ferry boats to get their goods to the other side of the river.

The original Blackwall Tunnel, the western bore, or 'old tunnel', was built between the years 1892 and 1897, well before the motor car was popular. In fact, in its early years, pedestrians and horse riders were the main patrons. Horse and carts also travelled through it, transferring cargos between the docks on either side of the river. The route curves sharply at either end, rumour has it, to calm horses who might bolt upon seeing daylight at either end! It was opened on 22 May 1897 by Queen Victoria's oldest son, the Prince of Wales.

The second tunnel, the eastern bore, or 'new tunnel', was opened in 1967 after vehicle numbers using the old tunnel rose to unmanageable numbers. At first, both tunnels were bi-directional if demand merited it. This was usually in the morning rush hour when most traffic was coming into London from the south towards the City. This resulted in the new tunnel being opened for northbound traffic as well as the old tunnel. However, after Transport for London banned bi-driectional use, traffic now travels northbound in the original tunnel and southbound in the newer tunnel. The old tunnel is 1,476 yards/1,350 metres long, whilst the new tunnel is 1,284 yards/1,174 metres long. Both tunnels have a 30 mph speed limit. There are plans to bring in a toll charge in the near future.

The southern entrance to the original Blackwall Tunnel. Note the traffic lights and height enforcement poles. (Wendy Chatterton)

Brynglas Tunnels, M4, Newport, Gwent

The Brynglas Tunnels are two bored tunnels situated to the north-west of Newport in Gwent, carrying the M4 motorway in two dual carriageways under the Crindau Ridge. As far back as 1946 plans were formulated to build a tunnel here as a way of easing congestion on Newport's roads. Back then a single tunnel was proposed, but these plans were eventually dropped. In 1959 the Newport Corporation put forward new plans which were finally approved by the Department of Transport in 1961. Work began the following year using traditional boring methods and the two tunnels were eventually opened to traffic in May 1967. There is no hard shoulder in the tunnels and, as the three lanes (in each direction) of the M4 motorway have to be funneled into two lanes here, the tunnels are often a source of congestion. This has led for calls for extra tunnels to be built on either side of the existing tunnels. The tunnels are 394 yards/360 metres in length and there is a variable speed limit for vehicles using the tunnels.

Chestfield Tunnel, A299, near Whitstable, Kent

The Chestfield Tunnel is on the A299, Thanet Way which runs from the end of the M2, east of Faversham through to Ramsgate Docks. The tunnel was opened in 1998 along with the A299 dual carriageway and takes the road underneath the Chestfield Golf Course. Work started on the tunnel in 1995, using the cut-and-cover method, with approximately 2 metres of earth covering the tunnel, which makes it one of the shallowest gaps between tunnel and surface in Britain. It is 344 yards/315 metres in length.

The Brynglas Tunnel entrance looking west. (Wendy Chatterton)

The Chestfield Tunnel in Kent looking west. (Wendy Chatterton)

Clyde Tunnel, A739, Glasgow

The Clyde Tunnel, situated to the west of Glasgow on the A739, connects Govan in the south with Whiteinch in the north. The idea of building a road tunnel under the River Clyde was one that had begun in the 1800s with the building of the Finnieston Harbour Tunnel in 1896. This was hardly ideal with motor vehicles having to be moved down to the tunnel by hydraulic lifts. A new road tunnel crossing the River Clyde further west

The northern entrance/exit of the Clyde Tunnel. Note the 30 mph speed limit.

was mooted soon after the Second World War, but it wasn't until 1957 that construction work actually started. This was due to lack of finance being available after the war and disagreements about where the tunnel would actually be sited.

The tunnel was constructed using a tunnel shield, with a gap of 6 metres being maintained below the riverbed. There are two separate bores carrying traffic in dual carriageways in either direction under the river. The northbound tunnel was formally opened on 3 July 1963 by Queen Elizabeth II, with the southbound tunnel being opened in March 1964. Each bore has a length of 833 yards/762 metres with a gradient of 1 in 16 from the entrance to its nadir. There is also a separate pedestrian/cycle walkway running parallel to the road tunnel.

On 21 September 1975 a bomb exploded in the pedestrian tunnel planted by members of the so called 'Tartan Army', a Scottish independence group. In 2013 to mark the fiftieth anniversary of its opening, HRH Princess Anne attended a ceremony to remember all the workers who built the tunnel, including two men who died during its construction. The tunnel now carries an estimated 25 million vehicles a year through it.

Conwy Tunnel, A55, near Conwy, Gwynedd

The Conwy Tunnel carries the A55 – the North Wales Expressway – under the River Conwy as a by-pass for the market town of Conwy on the western bank of the river;

The eastern entrance to the Conwy Tunnel. Note the signs in both English and Welsh. (Wendy Chatterton)

a notorious bottleneck for traffic travelling along the A55. The tunnel is 1,192 yards/1,090 metres long, making it the longest road tunnel in Wales and it is unusal in that it was the first of the immersed tube tunnel variety to be used in Britain. Work on the £190 million tunnel started in September 1986, with the tunnel being constructed using three different sections. In constructing the tunnel, the central immersed tube section was floated into position and placed on the estuary bed. The western and eastern sections were then joined to this central section and then finally the roadway was put in. The tunnel was opened in October 1991 by Queen Elizabeth II. In January and February 2015, the lighting system in the tunnel was updated. The tunnel has a 70 mph speed limit.

Cuilfail Tunnel, A26, Lewes, East Sussex

The Cuilfail Tunnel (pronounced 'Kool Fale'), is a 459 yards/420 metres long tunnel, situated to the east of Lewes town centre. It runs under the chalk-based Cliffe Hill and was contructed using the boring method. It is on the A26 (Maidstone to Newhaven road), which joins up with the A27 (Brighton to Eastbourne road) to the south-east of Lewes. The tunnel was built as a way of taking traffic away from the historic town centre of Lewes, with plans for a by-pass road going back to before the Second World War. Previous plans had seen a proposed tunnel running underneath Cliffe High Street to Morris Road.

The Lewes side of the Cuilfail Tunnel in West Sussex. Note the fossil sculpture on the roundabout by the entrance.

The local campaign group The Friends of Lewes had campaigned against this in two public inquiries in 1964 and 1972. Construction of the A26/A27 bypass eventually started in 1975, with work on the tunnel starting in 1978. The tunnel was officially opened on 1 December 1980 by P. Gladwin, the Chairman of East Sussex County Council.

The name of the tunnel comes from the housing development on the hill the tunnel goes under. The estate's developer, a Mr Isaac Vinall, is said to have taken the name 'Cuilfail' from his favourite hill in his native Scotland. 'Cuilfail' is a Gaelic word which means either 'Sheltered Corner' or 'Paul's Retreat' depending upon which source you believe! At the northern entrance to the tunnel on a roundabout, the 'Cuilfail Spiral', a stone sculpture by Peter Randall-Page, is situated. It depicts a giant ammonite fossil and is made up of seven pieces of Portland limestone. It was placed there in 1983 and is known locally as 'Brian the Snail'.

Dartford Tunnels, A282, Dartford, Kent/Thurrock, Essex

The Dartford Tunnels are two parallel tunnels on the A282 which pass under the River Thames between Dartford in Kent and Thurrock in Essex. Together with the Queen Elizabeth Bridge, they make up the 'Dartford Crossing'. The first tunnel was opened in

1963, whilst the second tunnel opened in 1980. They are both 1-mile/1.61 kilometres in length and signs on the Kent side dsiplay this just before the tunnel entrances.

Plans for a tunnel crossing of the River Thames at this location were first proposed in 1924, but it wasn't until 1936 that pilot holes were dug. This was followed by more deeper bore holes in 1938, though with the advent of the Second World War, work was abandoned for many years. In fact, it wasn't until 1955 that work started again and the two original bore holes were eventually joined up under the Thames on 19 April 1959. However, the construction of the tunnel was further delayed by disputes about which roads the tunnel would link to. It was planned to link the tunnel to the North and South Orbital roads, which would traverse the outer limits of Greater London. These came to be known as 'Ringway 3', an orbital road round the edge of London which would later evolve into the M25.

It wasn't until the early 1960s that concerns about the route were resolved and the first tunnel was eventually opened in November 1963. This tunnel cost £13 million and it was estimated that there would be 2 million vehicles a year using it. However, due to its popularity and it being the only river crossing of the Thames between Essex and Kent, a second tunnel was soon called for. Work was started in 1972 with completion due for 1976. However, the public enquiry into this second tunnel delayed work, so it wasn't actually opened until 1980. This time the cost was £45 million, with an expected capacity of 65,000 vehicles per day. When the M25 was completed in 1986 and more traffic began using the tunnels, a third crossing was called for and so the Queen Elizabeth Bridge was built next to the tunnels, opening in 1991.

The entrance to the first Dartford Tunnel. Note the air vents directly above the entrance and the Dartford Bridge beyond that. (Wendy Chatterton)

This led to the two tunnels being used for northbound traffic, while the bridge was used for southbound traffic. These tunnels are among the busiest road tunnels in Britain, with road links to the two ends of the M25. On occasions, when high winds occur and the bridge is shut, traffic uses the newer tunnel southbound from Essex into Kent. There has always been a toll charge at this crossing of the Thames. The actual repayment cost of the tunnel and bridge was completed in 2003, yet the toll charge has remained. Public opinion against the toll led to the crossing being free to motorists between 10.00 p.m. and 6.00 a.m. and free for motorcyclists at all times. The toll booths were removed in October 2014 and cameras now record all vehicles using the crossing.

East India Dock Road Tunnel, A13/A1261, Tower Hamlets, London

This tunnel in London's Docklands was built as part of the regeneration of the Docklands area. It links the A13 in the east with the A1261 at its western end, which in turn connects with the Limehouse Link Tunnel. Its purpose was to help traffic avoid the bottleneck of the roundabout at Leamouth Road, the A1020, which it passes under and so speed up traffic going into and out of the City of London. Work commenced on the tunnel in November 1990 and the tunnel was first opened to traffic in May 1993, though only in the westbound direction. It was built using the cut-and-cover method and is approximately 380 yards/350 metres in length.

The East India Dock Road Tunnel looking at its western entrance where it separates from Aspen Way.

The northern entrance to the Eastway Tunnel in Hackney, East London.

Eastway Tunnel, A12, Hackney, London

The Eastway Tunnel is a dual carriageway tunnel on the A12 in East London and one of three major tunnels on this section of the A12. The name 'Eastway' comes from the 'Eastway Road Scheme', which was meant to be the East London equivalent of the Westway in West London, taking fast traffic into and out of central London from the east, as part of the defunct 'Ringways' scheme. This tunnel is unusual in that it is only one directional, i.e. the route goes from north to south, with no equivalent south to north tunnel. It is one of the earliest road tunnels to be built in this part of London and was opened in 1974. It has a length of 317 yards/290 metres.

Eltham Tunnel, A2, Eltham, Greenwich, London

The Eltham Tunnel in South East London carries the A2 Rochester Way Relief Road under the A208, Well Hall Road and Eltham bus station, which is next to Eltham railway station. In 1985 the two railway stations in Eltham – Eltham Park and Eltham Well Hall – were closed and replaced with one new main station between the two, simply called 'Eltham'. This was partly to fit in with the new Rochester Way Relief Road being built to the

The Eltham Tunnel looking west with the Eltham Bus Interchange above it.

south of the railway line. This dual carriageway was designed to bring traffic from South East London and Kent through Eltham on a by-pass and on into central London via the Blackwall Tunnel. As a result, the new road went underneath the new Eltham bus station in a short tunnel. The tunnel is approximately 185 yards/170 metres long and was built using the cut-and-cover method. Several houses had to be demolished to make way for the new road and station.

Fore Street Tunnel, A406, Edmonton, Enfield, London

The Fore Street Tunnel is situated on the A406 North Circular Road in the district of Edmonton in North London. It carries the North Circular Road under the Angel Edmonton Interchange where the A1010, Fore Street, crosses over the A406 North Circular Road. Silver Street railway station on the London Liverpool Street to Cheshunt line also goes over the tunnel. It was constructed using the cut-and-cover method and was opened in 1998 to help the North Circular Road avoid this road junction. It is approximately 380 yards/350 metres in length. In 2015 the tunnel was refurbished after a problem of leaking water had been identified, which was damaging some of the electrical equipment in the tunnel.

The Fore Street Tunnel on the North Circular Road in North London looking west.

George Green Tunnel, A12, Wanstead, Redbridge, London

This is another of the three major road tunnels on the A12 dual carriageway in East London and it is situated in the district of Wanstead. It is named after the area of open land through which part of the tunnel goes under. It was decided to build a tunnel as opposed to a road next to the green, which would have disturbed the area more. It became the scene of one of the first major road protests in Britain, involving hundreds of protestors. This was because the tunnel engineers had opted for constructing the tunnel using the cut-and-cover method as opposed to boring. The construction of the tunnel involved the digging up of part of the green and in particular the felling of a 250-year-old chestnut tree.

The 'M11 Link Road', as it was then called, would go under the green and this was given the final go-ahead in 1989, but it was several years before construction work began. This was because of protests by activists who were against the road. The protestors used an ancient chestnut tree on George Green as their central hub. Some of them started living in 'The Tree' and in some derelict houses on the route. The police eventually managed to dislodge the protestors in December 1993, but it would be over six years before the road and tunnel were finally opened. Many see this protest as the start of large-scale environmental protests in other parts of the country whenever a new road was planned. The tunnel was eventually opened in 2000 and is approximately 275 yards/250 metres in length.

The George Green Tunnel in North East London looking north. Note the tower of Wanstead London Underground station beyond the tunnel.

The Gibraltar Hill Tunnels on the A40 near Monmouth, South Wales, looking southwards.

Gibraltar Hill Tunnels, A40, Monmouth, Monmouthshire

This pair of bored tunnels were opened in 1967 and carry the A40 under Gibraltar Hill to the south of the ancient town of Monmouth. The tunnel was built under Gibraltar Hill to form a by-pass around Monmouth for the A40 trunk road, which connects Cardiff to the south with the M50 and M5 motorways to the north. Prior to the building of the tunnels the A40 passed through the centre of Monmouth, so when the route was changed the best option was to bore a tunnel under the hill. The tunnels opened in 1966 and are approximately 200 yards/183 metres long. The work took two years to complete. There is a 50 mph speed limit in the tunnels.

Green Man Tunnel, A12, Leytonstone, Waltham Forest, London

This is another of the three major road tunnels on the A12 in East London. It is named after a local public house and roundabout in the district of Leytonstone. There have been several 'Green Man' pubs on this site going as far back as the 1600s, though the pub lost its 'Green Man' name in 1995. However, the roundabout at this location retains the name of the Green Man Roundabout, as does the tunnel. The Green Man Tunnel was opened in 2000 as a dual carriageway with twin bores and is approximately 185 yards/170 metres long. There is a 40 mph speed limit in the tunnels as the roadway curves quite noticeably inside. In 2014 the A12 in this part of East London was listed as being in the top twenty for congested roads in Europe.

The southern entrance to the Green Man Tunnel in North East London. Note the sharp bend by the tunnel entrance.

Hanger Lane Tunnel, Western Avenue, A40, Ealing, London

The Hanger Lane Tunnel goes underneath the Hanger Lane Gyratory road junction in Ealing, West London, which is one of the busiest road junctions in Britain. This carries the A406 North Circular Road over the A40 trunk road and the Central Line London Underground route. The Hanger Lane Gyratory System came into being as a result of the building of a complete roundabout, where the A406 North Circular Road dualled section changed into a single section at this interchange. The A4005, Hanger Lane also joins this junction from the north. The tunnel was opened as long ago as 1960 and cost almost £1 million pounds after several delays. Work was started in June 1958 with a completion date set for March 1960. The tunnel did not open until October 1960 due to a labour shortage. It is approximately 280 yards/260 metres long and carries over 20 million vehicles through it each year. In 2012 a new fire protection system was built in the tunnel, due to the asbestos used in the building of the tunnel starting to escape as a result of water ingression. The whole of the tunnel casing was treated to stop this happening.

The westbound entrance to the Hanger Lane Tunnel. (Graham Upwey)

The Hatfield Tunnel looking north with the Galleria Shopping Centre above it. (Wendy Chatterton)

Hatfield Tunnel, A1(M), Hatfield, Hertfordshire

The Hatfield Tunnel houses the A1(M) in Hertfordshire as it goes under the Galleria Shopping Centre in Hatfield. It is 1312 yards/1200 metres long and was opened on 10 December 1986 by the Duke of Kent after three years of construction work. This involved demolishing existing buildings, constructing the tunnel using the cut-and-cover method and building the A1(M) motorway along this route. The tunnel was built to join up with the A1(M) both north and south of Hatfield, which had not been constructed through Hatfield. Joining this missing link with a tunnel was seen as the best option. After the tunnel was completed, the area above the tunnel became the Galleria Shopping Centre at its south end, and the centre car park and the Hatfield Garden village roundabout at its northern end. Due to the incidence of ground water in this area, drainage pumps were built into the tunnel infrastructure, carrying the water away from the tunnel and into local rivers.

Hindhead Tunnel, A3, Hindhead, Surrey

The Hindhead Tunnel in Surrey is one of the newest road tunnels in Great Britain. It was built on the A3 London to Portsmouth trunk road, which is dual carriageway for most of its length. The main exception to this was the notorious Devil's Punch Bowl at Hindhind, which caused endless delays as traffic went around the edge of this Area of Outstanding Natural Beauty with a 30 mph speed limit. That part of the road has now been complely removed and has reverted back to open moorland under the guardianship of the National Trust.

Looking down at the Hindhead Tunnel southern entrance from Miss James Bridge.

The 4-mile-long by-pass of Hindhead, which includes the tunnel, was opened in July 2011 at a total cost of £371 million. It is a state-of-the-art road tunnel, complete with the most up to date saftey features and signs showing the variable speed limit and warnings of any problems ahead. The rocks that were dug out from the tunnel were used to level out the old road around the Devil's Punch Bowl. The tunnel was dug out using mechanical diggers as opposed to a boring machine and is 1.14 miles/1.83 kilometres in length, making it the longest road tunnel under land in Great Britain and the third longest overall.

Holmesdale Tunnel, M25, Cheshunt, Hertfordshire/Enfield, London

The Holmesdale tunnel on the M25 motorway is situated just to the east of Junction 25 and is on the border of Hertfordshire and Enfield, in North London. Its name comes from a street called 'Holmesdale' in Enfield, which is above the tunnel. Originally there were several glass houses in this area which provided fruit and vegetables for London. After the Second World War these were mostly demolished and new housing was put up. A strip of wasteland, known locally as 'the Backfield', remained between Cameron Drive in Waltham Cross, Hertfordshire, to the north, and Holmesdale in Enfield, Greater London, to the south. Basically, it divided Enfield from Waltham Cross. It was a popular piece of recreation

The eastern entrance to the Holmesdale Tunnel on the M25. (Wendy Chatterton)

ground for both communities and when planners wanted to build the M25 through this gap near the River Lee, it was eventually agreed that a cut-and-cover tunnel under this area would be the best option.

Work on the tunnel began in 1981 and was completed in 1984, which meant that the M25 was now continuous from the north side of the Dartford Tunnel, in Essex, as far as the A1(M) in Hertfordshire. However, it would be another two years before the M25 was completed.

The cost of the tunnel was just under £30 million, making this the most expensive piece of roadway ever built at the time. The tunnel was originally 733 yards/670 metres long and there were three lanes in each direction with a hard shoulder and raised walkways. However, only two lanes were for through traffic, with the third lane being for traffic exiting or entering the A10 at Junction 25. As time went on there were often jams at busy periods, so the hard shoulder and raised walkways were removed in the early 2000s to allow for three lane running, both in the tunnel and through Junction 25. At the same time, the outdated ventilation and drainage systems were renewed, with all mechanical and electrical equipment being replaced. Finally, the tunnels were extended by 37 yards/ 34 metres at both ends to house new ventilation systems.

Kingsway Tunnel, A59, Wallasey/Liverpool, Merseyside

The Kingsway Tunnel carries the A59 between Livepool in the north and Wallasey in the south, running under the River Mersey. It was built to relieve the congestion of the original Mersey Tunnel and to help move traffic coming into Liverpool from the Wirral away from Liverpool town centre and towards the north. Work on the tunnel started in 1966 and was finished eight years later in 1974. Although the entrances make it look like one large tunnel, there are in fact two separate bores. These were dug out by a large boring machine nicknamed the 'Mersey Mole'. The tunnel was formally opened on 24 June 1971 by Queen Elizabeth II, though at this stage only the southern tube was

The Kingsway or Wallasey Tunnel looking north towards Liverpool.

actually open. It wasn't until February 1974 that the northern tube was completed and opened to traffic. The tunnel cost almost £20 million to build and eight men died during its construction. Their names were listed on memorial plaques erected at either end of the tunnel in 1997. The tunnel is approximately 1.5 miles/2.4 kilometres in length, making it the second longest road tunnel in Great Britain. A toll is in force with toll booths being sited on the Wallasey side. It is called the 'Wallasey Tunnel' by many locals and local street signage also shows this.

Limehouse Link Tunnel, Limehouse/Poplar, Tower Hamlets, London

The Limehouse Link Tunnel in East London carries the A1203 from the north of Canary Wharf, in the east, going under Ropemakers Fields and Limehouse Basin, before emerging just before the Rotherhithe Tunnel, in Limehouse, in the west. It is the longest road tunnel in London and the fourth longest in Britain, coming in at 1.19 miles/1.91 kilometres long. It was built to relieve the large amount of congestion in this part of East London and to provide a quicker route between the City of London and the Canary Wharf complex. Work started in November 1989, and the tunnel was opened on 17 May 1993 as part of several new road schemes in the Docklands area of East London, which was then being redeveloped. The tunnel was constructed by the cut-and-cover method and its cost was £293 million making it the most expensive stretch of road per mile in Britain to date. The tunnel is quite unusual in that it has a second entrance/exit for Westferry Road, not far from the eastern entrance to the tunnel. This is to give access to Canary Wharf. Above each of the four entrances/exits to the tunnel can be found various works of modern art. After a series of road traffic accidents in the tunnel the speed limit was reduced from 70 mph to 30 mph, which is enforced by average speed cameras.

The Western portal of the Limehouse Link Tunnel in Limehouse. Note the artwork above the tunnel entrance which is by Zadok Ben-David and called *Restless Dream.*

The northern end of the Matthew Murray Tunnel in Leeds. (Wendy Chatterton)

Matthew Murray Tunnel, A643, Leeds, West Yorkshire

The Matthew Murray Tunnel in Leeds is a 175 yards/160 metres long twin bore road tunnel on the A643 Ingram Road Distributor, which takes traffic into and out of the city centre from the M621, which in turn links with the M62. It is named after the Matthew Murray School whose grounds the tunnel originally went under. The tunnel was built in the 1970s and was designed to minimise noise from the road disrupting the school and its grounds above the tunnel. Originally the A463 was to have gone right through the grounds and, after local opposition, a tunnel was deemed the best option. The school was named after Matthew Murray, one of the founding fathers of Leeds, who was instrumental in setting up many of the early woollen mills in and around Leeds. The school was demolished in 2007, though there is still open land above the tunnel.

The westbound entrance and eastbound exit of the Medway Tunnel in Chatham, Kent.

Medway Tunnel, A289, Chatham, Kent

The Medway Tunnel in Kent was opened on 12 June 1996 by the Princess Royal. It is part of the A289 Medway Towns Northern Relief Road and links Chatham in the east with Strood in the west. The tunnel is 262 yards/240 metres long and goes under the River Medway to the north of Rochester. It is split into three distinct sections – two cut-and-cover tunnels under the west and east banks of the river and an immersed tube which has been placed on the riverbed. The ownership of the tunnel is quite interesting with the tunnel being owned by the Rochester Bridge Trust, who also own the two bridges going over the River Medway on the A2 road. They own the freehold of the tunnel, but since 2008 Medway Council has a 999-year lease on the tunnel and is now responsible for its day to day running and maintenance.

Meir Tunnel, A50 Stoke-on-Trent, Staffordshire

The Meir Tunnel in Stoke-on-Trent, Staffordshire, takes the A50 dual carriageway under the A520, Weston Road, in the district of Meir in Stoke. The tunnel was the result of the A50 road in Stoke being converted into a dual carriageway in the 1990s. Originally there were plans to have a flyover at this junction, but local opposition led to a tunnel being built instead. The whole scheme cost £125 million and led to many homes being demolished. The tunnel section itself coast £18 million and work began in April 1995. The tunnel was built using the cut-and-cover method and is 311 yards/284 metres long. It was first opened to road vehicles on 28 November 1997, though the whole scheme was not completed until 1998. 1998, the year the tunnel was completed, can be seen in bricks above the western entrance to the tunnel. At the eastern entrance there is the coat of arms of Stoke-on-Trent City Council, along with a rope design showing the Stafford Knot. Inside are the hands of the potter and the fire of industry. On either side of the knot can be seen the tools of the potter. In 2013 the old fluorescent lighting system in the tunnel was refurbished with LED lights installed in their place.

The western entrance to the Meir Tunnel on the A50 in Stoke-on-Trent. (Wendy Chatterton)

The western entrance of the main Pen-y-Clip tunnel on the A55 in North Wales.

Pen-y-Clip Tunnels, A55, Penmaenmawr, Gwynedd

The Pen-y-Clip tunnels are a group of three tunnels on the A55 North Wales Expressway, situated to the west of Penmaenmawr in the county of Gwynedd. There are two short tunnels, approximately 33 yards/30 metres long, on the westbound carriageway of the A55, which were opened in 1935 when the road was realigned. This section of the road here carried two-way traffic and clung to the side of the cliff which jutted out into the sea. The tunnels were bored out of two rock outcrops which stood in the way of the road and look almost identical. The A55 continued using this route until the 1990s when increasing traffic numbers led to a third tunnel being built right through the base of the headland known as Penmaenan Point. This tunnel, which opened in 1993, carried a new dual carriageway through the mountain in a bored tunnel, which took three and a half years to construct. This third tunnel is 1,017 yards/ 930 metres long and carries westbound traffic, while the other two tunnels now carry eastbound traffic. If necessary, either roadway can be used for bi-directional traffic when one of the tunnels has to be closed for maintenance.

The western entrance to the Penmaenbach Tunnel westbound bore. (Wendy Chatterton)

Penmaenbach Tunnels, A55, Penmaenmawr, Gwynedd

The Penmaenbach Tunnels are on the A55, to the east of Penmaenmawr in North Wales, and get their name from the Penmaenbach Headland which they go under. The shorter tunnel, carrying eastbound traffic in two lanes, was opened in 1932 as part of the newly aligned A55 and is approximately 185 yards/170 metres long. There is a 30 mph speed limit here as the road curves quite sharply following the contours of the headland. The other longer tunnel was opened in 1989 and carries westbound traffic towards Bangor on a dual carriageway. It is 726 yards/664 metres long. There is a wide gap between the two tunnels as the possibility of building a straighter, eastbound tunnel at a later date may eventually happen. In 2015 the lighting in the westbound tunnel was replaced with LED lighting to comply with European safety standards for road tunnels.

Queen's Gate Tunnel, A4232, Cardiff, South Glamorgan

The Queen's Gate Tunnel in Cardiff is a 793-yard/725-metre long twin bore tunnel carrying the A4232 under the Butetown area of Cardiff. The road in this part of Cardiff is called the Butetown Link Road and the tunnel is locally known as 'the Butetown Tunnel'. The whole road is designed to link the M4 and A48(M) in the east with south and west Cardiff in a dual carriageway, which again links up with the M4 in the west. South Glamorgan County Council had originally planned to build an elevated section of the road through Butetown, but local residents and the Cardiff Bay Development Corporation protested against this, as it would split the community in half, and the plans were changed to having a tunnel instead. Costs went from £35 million to £45 million, mainly as a result of this cut-and-cover tunnel being added to the origin plans. The tunnel was opened in 1996 and now carries over 16 million vehicles through it annually. The tunnel has been used as a location for both the *Dr Who* and *Torchwood* TV shows. In the 2009 *Dr Who* episode the tunnel was called the 'Gladwell Tunnel'.

The Queens Gate Tunnel in Cardiff looking at the eastbound carriageway. (Wendy Chatterton)

The northbound entrance to the Rotherhithe Tunnel in South London. Note the pavement for pedestrians.

Rotherhithe Tunnel, A101, Limehouse, Tower Hamlets/Rotherhithe, Southwark, London

One of the oldest road tunnels still open in London is the Rotherhithe Tunnel, which was opened in 1908 by the then Prince of Wales; just over ten years after the nearby Blackwall Tunnel. Like that tunnel, it was built to carry goods between the docks situated on either side of the River Thames. It connects Limehouse in the north with Rotherhithe in the south and is 1,621 yards/1,482 metres long. The unusual thing about the Rotherhithe Tunnel is that pedestrians are allowed to walk through the tunnel if they so wish, as there are pavements on both sides of the tunnel. It is believed that a handful of people a day still do so, though it is not to be encouraged due to the traffic fumes. Cyclists are also allowed to ride through the tunnel. Partly due to this there is a 20 mph speed limit, which is the slowest speed limit for any of the major road tunnels in Britain. When it was first opened, horse traffic, rather than motor vehicles, was the dominant form of transport. It is believed that the feature of having sharp bends at either end in its end was to calm horses that might bolt when they saw the light at the end of the tunnel.

Roundhill Tunnel, A20, Folkestone, Kent

The Roundhill Tunnel to the north of Folkestone, carries the A20 dual carriageway under Roundhill, a chalk outcrop, and onto the port of Dover. It was built at the same time as the Channel Tunnel in the 1990s as part of the Channel Tunnel road's infrastructure. As such, it links the British end of the Channel Tunnel with the port of Dover. It consists of a pair of twin bored tunnels which are linked to the Castle Hill Interchange and the M20 by a viaduct. The tunnel opened on 8 December 1993 and is approximately 415 yards/380 metres long. The New Austrian Tunnelling Method (NATM) was used in the building of the tunnel due to the unpredictability of the chalk through which the tunnel was bored.

Royal Harbour Tunnel, A299, Ramsgate, Kent

The Royal Harbour Tunnel or simply 'Ramsgate Tunnel' is an 875 yards/800 metres long tunnel cut into the chalk cliffs to the south-west of Ramsgate. It carries the A299 as the Royal Harbour Approach Road down through the cliff to the port of Ramsgate. It was built to take traffic away from the narrow streets of the town and straight to the docks area. The original plans were for a much shorter and shallower tunnel, but these were changed to stop several residents of the Pegwell area losing their homes and the need to avoid disturbing electrical and sewer pipe work. The tunnel was opened in 2000 and is sometimes known as the 'Pegwell Tunnel' after the area of Ramsgate that it goes under.

Saltash Tunnel, A38, Saltash, Cornwall

The Saltash Tunnel in Cornwall carries the A38 under the town of Saltash, in east Cornwall, and is situated immediately to the west of the Tamar Bridge, which links Devon with Cornwall. The tunnel is 448 yards/410 metres long and was opened in 1988 by Paul Channon, the then Transport Secretary. The tunnel is unusual in that it has three lanes, with the middle lane being reversible, according to traffic conditions; the same as the roadway over the Tamar Bridge. When the tunnel was first opened, water ingress soon became a problem due to the chalk rocks being highly saturated. Remedial work took place which relined the tunnel in a £7.4 million project. More recently in 2018/19 the tunnel has had heat and smoke detector systems installed, as well as new emergency evacuation signs.

The Roundhill Tunnel in Folkestone as it goes under Roundhill looking east. (Wendy Chatterton)

Looking down on the southern portal of the Royal Harbour Tunnel in Ramsgate Kent.

The eastern portal of the Saltash Tunnel in Cornwall with its unusual three lanes.

The twin portals of the Southwick Hill Tunnel in West Sussex looking west. (Wendy Chatterton)

Southwick Hill Tunnel, A27, Mile Oak, West Sussex

The Southwick Hill Tunnel on the A27 in West Sussex is a twin bore tunnel, which opened on 18 March 1996. The tunnel was built using the New Austrian Tunnelling Method due to the unpredictability of the chalk through which the tunnel was bored. This and poor weather conditions led to delays in the date of the tunnel's opening, as well as causing the tunnel to come in over budget. A tunnel was chosen, as opposed to a cutting, in order to preserve the natural landscape above, much of which belongs to the National Trust. The tunnel is also known locally as the Southwick Tunnel and each bore is approximately 425 yards/390 metres long.

Tyne Tunnel, A19, Jarrow/Howden, Newcastle upon Tyne, Tyne and Wear

The two Tyne tunnels on the A19 go under the River Tyne 7 miles to the east of Newcastle upon Tyne, connecting Howden and North Shields in the north with Jarrow in the south. It was as long ago as 1937 that a road tunnel was proposed by the then Durham and Northumberland county councils. Before the original road tunnel was built a separate pedestrian and cyclist tunnel was constructed with work starting in 1947 and completion happening in 1951. It was another ten years before work started on the original Tyne road tunnel though, with the tunnel being dug out using a tunnelling shield. It was finally opened on 19 October 1967 by Queen Elizabeth II, but didn't become operational until the following year, once the northern link roads had been finished. It was designed to take 25,000 vehicles a day but by 2000 it was carrying 35,000 vehicles a day, with long queues at peak times.

In March 2004 a second tunnel was announced by the Tyne and Wear Integrated Transport Authority at a cost of £139 million. Work started in the Spring of 2008 and was completed in less than three years. This time an immersed tube was used in the construction of the tunnel. The final cost was in the region of £260 million. Once remedial work on the original tunnel had been completed, the traffic flow was changed so that northbound traffic would use the original tunnel and southbound traffic would use the new tunnel, with two lanes in each tunnel. Queen Elizabeth II returned to the North East to open the new tunnel on 18 July 2012, which had been open to traffic from February 2011 onwards. The original Tyne Tunnel is 1-mile/1,700 metres long while the newer tunnel is approximately 0.9 miles/1,500 metres long. There is a toll to use the tunnel, with the toll booths being situated on the north side of the tunnel.

Weston Hills Tunnel, A505, Baldock, Hertfordshire

The Weston Hills Tunnel to the east of Baldock, Hertfordshire, carries the A505 Baldock by-pass in a twin bore tunnel under the Weston Hills area. It is a cut-and-cover tunnel which was opened on 16 March 2006, after construction began in April 2004. The tunnel is 251 yards/230 metres long and is part of a £43 million project to build the by-pass and tunnel around Baldock. A tunnel, as opposed to a cutting, was chosen to preserve both the landscape and the natural ecosystem of the area, which includes deer and butterflies.

Looking at the southern exit of the Tyne Tunnel on the A19 in Jarrow. (Nick Hartington)

The twin bores of the eastern entrance to the Weston Hills Tunnel in Hertfordshire. (Wendy Chatterton)

CHAPTER 2

Road Tunnels in City Centres

The tunnels and underpasses in this chapter can all be found in the city centre areas of the towns and cities listed below. Many of them are on ring roads which skirt around city centres helping the traffic to avoid going through them. Most of them were built from the 1960s onwards, a period of great redevelopment in many towns and cities throughout Britain, after bomb damage from the Second World War.

Birmingham

There are several tunnels and underpasses that can be found on the two ring roads, which run around Birmingham city centre. The original Inner Ring Road or Queensway was the A4400, or 'Concrete Collar' as it came to be known, and was the brainchild of Herbert Manzoni, the City Engineer and Surveyor of Birmingham from 1935 to 1963. This road incorporated various tunnels and underpasses but was superseded by the Middle Ring Road or 'Middleway' (the A4540), which again is a ring road, but about a mile further out from the city centre.

Five Ways Underpass

The Five Ways Roundabout, situated to the south-west of Birmingham city centre, is where the A546, coming out of Birmingham as Broad Street, meets the Birmingham Middle Ring Road and the start of the A456 Hagley Road. The underpass here goes under the Five Ways Roundabout, where it changes from Broad Street to Hagley Road. Since June 2019 it has been closed to traffic, while the roadway is changed to allow the tracks of the West Midlands Metro Tram to run through it.

Holloway Circus Underpass

This underpass runs underneath the Holloway Circus Roundabout as Queensway Suffolk Street. The A4040 goes south and changes to Queensway Bristol Street – the A38 – halfway under the intersection. On the roundabout above there is a 40-foot Chinese pagoda, which is a local landmark.

A lone car emerges out of the eastern bore of the Lancaster Circus Tunnel in Birmingham.

Lancaster Circus Tunnel
The Lancaster Circus Tunnel is situated on the A34 where it goes under the A38 Queensway just to the north of Birmingham city centre. It is noticeable for the colourful triangular murals on the side walls.

Lee Bank Middleway/Bellgrave Middleway
The underpass here is on the A4540 Lee Bank Middleway as it changes to the Bellgrave Middleway in the underpass. It crosses underneath the A38 Bristol Street, one junction south of the Holloway Circus Underpass nearer the city centre. It is approximately 55 yards/50 metres in length.

Queensway Tunnel
The Queensway Tunnel is the longest of the road tunnels in the centre of Birmingham with a length of 597 yards/546 metres. It was originally built to take the busy A38 traffic running from north to south, round the western edge of Birmingham city centre. Starting as Great Charles Street Queensway at its northern end, the tunnel becomes the A4400 as part of the Inner Ring Road. It originally went under Paradise Circus, Queensway Roundabout, where the A456 and A457 roads met on their way into the city centre. This junction has now been

Looking south into the northern entrance of the Queensway Tunnel in Birmingham.

redesigned as a pedestrianised area called 'Paradise' and the roads coming into it realigned. The tunnel emerges at its southern end as Suffolk Street Queensway and becomes the A38. The tunnel was built using the cut-and-cover method and was formally opened in 1971 by Queen Elizabeth II.

Saint Chad's Circus Tunnel

The St Chads Tunnel has its southern portal directly underneath the platforms of Birmingham Snow Hill station. It goes under St Chad's Circus roundabout, where the A41 passes above on its way into Birmigham city centre and emerges onto St Chad's Queensway. It is a twin bore tunnel on a dual carriageway, taking traffic round the western side of Birmingham city centre and has a length of 185 yards/169 metres.

Caernarvon

Caernarvon Tunnel, Caernarvon, Gwynedd

This tunnel was originally a railway tunnel carrying an 8-mile-long branch line from Llanberis to Caernarvon station. As Caernarvon station was to the north of the town centre, and the line came in from the south, a tunnel was needed to make the connection. The tunnel was closed in 1964 after passenger services had ceased in 1962. For many years the

The former railway tunnel in Caernarvon, North Wales, which is now used by road traffic. Note the castle on the left in the background.

tunnel lay derelict, but in 1995 the tunnel was opened to motor traffic, joining Bridge Street with St Helen's Road. It is a two-way tunnel and is about 300 yards/270 metres in length and has a 20 mph speed limit. It was used as a filming location for the BBC TV programme *Casualty*, as the setting for a major road traffic accident in a tunnel.

Coventry

Greyfriars Green Tunnel, A4053, Coventry, West Midlands
The Greyfriars Green Tunnel, as it is known locally in Coventry, carries the Inner Coventry Ring Road, the A4053, under Greyfriars Green – a popular area of open space to the south of Coventry city centre. Although the road was originally built in the 1960s, the tunnel was only recently opened in 2015, making it one of Britain's newest road tunnels. Previously at this junction there was an open roundabout with a graded exit. By building the tunnel using the cut-and-cover method, it meant that Greyfriars Green could be extended southwards towards Coventry railway station.

The tunnel at Greyfriars Green in Coventry shortly after it had been opened in 2015. Note the new area of grass on the top of the tunnel.

The Marketgait Tunnel in Dundee looking north with the town centre to the right.

The M8 goes under the Charing Cross Tunnel in Glasgow.

Dundee

Marketgait Tunnel, A991, Dundee

The Marketgait Tunnel in Dundee is situated to the north of the city centre on the Dundee Inner Ring Road – the A991. This dual carriageway road circumnavigates the city centre of Dundee. It was built in the years 1990 to 1992 and involved demolishing many houses. The tunnel is 159 yards/145 metres long and goes under Victoria Road and the Hilltown just to the north of the Wellgate shopping centre.

Glasgow

Charing Cross Tunnel, M8, Glasgow

The Charing Cross Tunnel in Glasgow carries the M8 motorway under the A804, Sauchiehall Street, and some areas of greenery, in a cut-and-cover tunnel. It is situated on the west side of the city centre, virtually next to Charing Cross railway station. This section of the M8 was opened in 1972 and is one of the busiest sections of motorway in Scotland. The tunnel carries six lanes of motorway into it, though a lane diverges from the northbound carriageway into a single-track tunnel, which eventually joins up with St George's Road, the A804. The tunnel is approximately 109 yards/100 metres in length and required many buildings to be demolished in this area of Glasgow during its construction.

Leeds

The Leeds Inner Ring Road, which runs from the west of the city centre around its northern perimeter and on to the east of the city centre, is a warren of road tunnels of varying lengths. Most of this road was built in the 1960s and 1970s following the demolition of old buildings along the road's route. It is also a combination of two urban motorways – the A58(M) and the A64(M) – which end and begin somewhere in the middle of this complicated road. Unlike most modern motorways, this road has junctions that enter and leave the motorway on its right side and some of the tunnels are only situated on one carriageway and not both. Here are the details of the six road tunnels along this road going from west to east.

West Street Tunnel

This is a one-way single tunnel which ends almost as soon as the Westgate Tunnel begins on the A58(M). It comes off West Street going north and at its end merges onto the A58(M) on its right. It is approximately 100 yards/91 metres long and was built with the cut-and-cover method in the 1970s. It runs only on the west side of the A58(M).

Westgate Tunnel

This short tunnel is on the A58(M) near its start, to the west of Leeds city centre and its name is often confused with the nearby Woodhouse Tunnel. The tunnel takes its name from the street called Westgate, which goes into Leeds city centre from the Park Lane Roundabout that this tunnel goes under. It is a dual carriage way tunnel with roads in both directions and was constructed using the cut-and-cover method.

The entrance to the West Street Tunnel in Leeds which is one way only.

The Woodhouse Tunnel, the longest road tunnel in Leeds with part of Leeds Infirmary on top.

Woodhouse Tunnel

A liitle further on from the Westgate Tunnel on the A58(M) is the Woodhouse Tunnel, which is the longest of all six road tunnels on the Inner Ring Road. Part of it goes under the Leeds General Infirmary and locals have been known to call this tunnel, the 'Infirmary Tunnel' because of this. It is 415 yards/380 metres long and was opened in 1964. In the years 2013–2016 an £11 million refurbishment of both bores of the tunnel took place. The work involved repairing the worn-out concrete, and reinforcing, waterproofing and renewing the drains.

Clay Pit Lane Junction Tunnels

There are three tunnels here running parallel with each other that go under the junction with the A58 Clay Pit Lane to the north of the city centre. They also mark the point where the A58(M) and the A64(M) start/end. The central carriageway has the main tunnel, while on either side two narrower tunnels carry joining roads onto/off the motorway.

North Street Junction Tunnel

This tunnel goes under North Street to the north of Leeds city centre. The eastbound tunnel leaves the main carriageway, which continues to a set of traffic lights above the tunnel. It does eventually join up with the westbound tunnel. It was built to take the Inner Ring Road under a complicated road layout above, which has five different directions of roadway.

Queuing traffic stretching all the way under the Southgates Underpass in Leicester. (Jim Chaucer)

New York Road Tunnel

This is an unusal tunnel layout with two different roads meeting together in the tunnel which runs directly underneath the New York Road Flyover. The tunnel goes on the west to east roadway only.

Leicester

Southgates Underpass, Vaughan Way, A594, Leicester, Leicestershire

The Southgates Underpass is situated just to the east of Leicester city centre and carries the A594 Vaughan Way under St Nicholas Place along the Leicester Central Ring. The underpass was constructed in the mid-1960s and opened in May 1968. It is about 325 yards/300 metres in length.

Liverpool

Queensway Tunnel, Liverpool/Birkenhead, Merseyside

The Queensway Tunnel, formerly called 'The Mersey Tunnel', runs between Liverpool and Birkenhead under the River Mersey and is Britain's longest road tunnel at just over 2 miles/3.24 kilometres long. It was built to connect the two places by road as the alternative was to take the ferry across the Mersey or to go by car via the nearest bridge crossing of the Mersey at Warrington, some twenty miles to the east. The tunnel was opened by King George V on 18 July 1934 in a ceremony attended by over 200,000 onlookers. The tunnel took nine years to build at a cost of £8 million and employed 1,700 men. During its construction, seventeen men were killed in various accidents and a memorial to them can be found on the side of the Georges Dock Building in Liverpool. There is also an original toll booth nearby. The tunnel is actually a tube with the current roadway built along the top half of the tube. The lower part was intended as a tramway, but due to the cost this plan was dropped. Today the lower half of the tunnel is used to carry pipes and cables and as an emergency escape route if needed.

Soon after it was opened, it came to be known as the 'eighth wonder of the world', as it was the longest road tunnel in the world at the time. It held this title for fourteen years, until it was superseded by the Vielha Tunnel in Spain. It is four lanes wide with no barrier or central reservation between the two carriageways. However, with safety to the forefront, there is now a 30 mph speed limit and heavy goods vehicles are banned from using it. Buses and vans must use the two centre lanes due to the low roof at the side. Another unusual thing about it is that it does not have a designated road number for it. It comes off the A41 on the Birkenhead side and the A59 on the Liverpool side. It also has its own dedicated police force, the Mersey Tunnels Police, along with its sister tunnel, the Kingsway Tunnel, between Liverpool and Wallasey.

For many years it was known as the 'Mersey Tunnel', but with the opening of the second tunnel under the River Mersey in 1971 between Liverpool and Wallasey, it came to be known locally as the 'Birkenhead Tunnel', or 'Old Tunnel'. Local street signs use this former

Traffic going into the Queensway Tunnel in Liverpool. Note the statues of King George V and Queen Mary on either side of the entrance.

designation, as opposed to the more formal name. The Queensway tunnel also has two other exits – one on each side of the river. The Liverpool exit comes out by the Liver Building on the waterfront and is still in use as an exit tunnel only. The Birkenhead exit was closed in 1965 due to congestion caused by traffic taking a right turn into it, but it is still used as a service tunnel. The Queensway Tunnel has always been a toll tunnel with toll booths being sited at either end. These are now just on the Birkenhead side. Finally, it is the only road tunnel in Great Britain where you can take a guided tour of it. This includes visiting the turbines used in tunnel ventilation, seeing the original control centre and walking under the tunnel itself.

London

London has several road tunnels and underpasses in and around its central area. These are listed in alphabetical order.

Beech Street Tunnel, Barbican, City of London

This unusual tunnel, which opened in 1969, is situated on the B100, Beech Street, between the A1 and the A501 in the City of London within the Barbican complex. It has a pavement on either side of the two-lane road and is possibly the most pedestrianised road tunnel

There seem to be more pedestrians than traffic in the Beech Street Tunnel in the City of London.

in Britain. The inner walls are paved with a mixture of white, cream, yellow, maroon and orange panels and it is brightly lit with hundreds of fluorescent lights in the ceiling.

It is just over 100 yards/91 metres in length and is called a 'pseudo-tunnel' by some people as it has several open sections at the sides, including the junction with Chiswell Street on its northern side. Plus, it has a thin roof covering, on top of which is a small park area, so it is not covered by another building. Recently it came third on a list of 'the most wretched streets in central London ranked by sheer awfulness' on the Londonist website. It has been used as the setting for several music videos including Kylie Minogue's *Giving You Up* and in some TV programmes including the BBC's *Ashes to Ashes.*

Hyde Park Corner Underpass, Kensington, London

Also known as 'the Piccadilly Underpass', this underpass carries traffic under the Hyde Park Corner Roundabout which is under the site of the Wellington Arch and the Australian War Memorial. It is on the A4, Piccadilly at the north-eastern tip of Green Park and just to the south-eastern corner of Hyde Park. It was officially opened in October 1962 by the then Duke of Wellingon and was built in response to the continuous traffic jams here. There were estimated to be 120,000 vehicles using the roundabout each day where Piccadilly met with Park Lane, Knightsbridge, Constitutional Hill and Grosvenor Place. The underpass is around 300 yards/274 metres in length and was constructed with the cut-and-cover method. It was refurbished in 2016 with the approaches to the tunnels clad in stainless steel panels and two 12-metre long advertising screens erected above the tunnel entrances. The western end of the tunnel marks the start of the Congestion Charge area for central London, and at either end are gates which can be moved across whenever the tunnel is shut.

Upper Thames Street Tunnel, Castle Banyard Street Tunnel, High Timber Street, City of London

This is a group of three tunnels all in the same structure on the Thames Embankment in Central London. The main tunnel, the Upper Thames Street Tunnel, carries the A3211 under various offices and the northern end of the Millenium Bridge. It was constructed in the 1960s when the whole road was widened, using the cut-and-cover method to build it. It is a dual carriageway road in two separate bores. On the north side of this main tunnel is Castle Banyard Tunnel, which is a one-way street going east, starting near Blackfriars railway station. It runs as a single roadway completely parallel to Upper Thames Street and then rejoins that road soon after the tunnel ends. Finally, there is what looks like a tunnel at High Timber Street at the eastern end of Upper Thames Street Tunnel. However, it does not emerge into daylight at the other end, instead ending at an underground entrance to one of the sets of offices above it.

A view looking down Upper Thames Street to the three tunnels which go under the office block in the picture. They are (from left to right) – High Timber Street, Upper Thames Street and Castle Banyard Street.

A lone motorcyclist emerges from the Strand Underpass onto Kingsway in Central London. (Colin Shepperton)

Strand Underpass, A301/A4200, Kingsway, London

This interesting road tunnel in central London was formerly used by trams. It is usually known as 'The Strand Underpass', though its alternative name is 'The Kingsway Tunnel'. It was first opened to road traffic in 1964, after having been used by trams as part of the Kingsway Tramway Subway. It is quite a narrow tunnel and begins at the northern end of Waterloo Bridge, going one-way northwards under The Strand and coming out in Kingsway.

Newcastle upon Tyne

A167(M), Newcastle upon Tyne, Tyne and Wear

There are two underpasses on the A167(M) in Newcastle upon Tyne that are situated to the north of the Tyne Bridge, which brings traffic into the city from Gateshead and further south. The motorway was built between the years 1972 and 1975 and was originally named the 'Central Motorway East'. It was designated the A1(M) to begin with but changed to the A6127(M), and then finally the A167(M). As an urban motorway built in the 1970s, it does not have a hard shoulder and some exits go off on the right-hand side. It is the only part still remaining of a much larger network of urban motorways that were planned to move traffic around the centre of Newcastle. Due to escalating costs and political changes in the city, the other planned motorways never came to fruition.

Today the A167(M) starts straight after the Tyne Bridge north of the River Tyne, and at its junction with the A186 goes under a local radio station in an underpass. Half a mile farther on there is another underpass, where the motorway goes under the roundabout where the A193 intersects with the motorway. The motorway continues as a dual carriageway to its end at Jesmond.

Stirling

Burghmuir Road Tunnel, A9, Stirling

The Burghmuir Road Tunnel, as it is known locally, is situated on the A9 in Stirling, just to the east of the town centre. It is a 100 yards/91 metres long cut-and-cover tunnel carrying the A9 dual carriageway under Station Road which leads to the front entrance of Stirling railway station.

The A167(M) goes under the A193 in an underpass to the east of Newcastle upon Tyne.

The underpass on the A9 that goes under Station Road in Stirling looking south.

CHAPTER 3

Road Tunnels at Airports

There are a number of tunnels based in or near six different airports in England, which have road tunnels running under them. These can be either tunnels running underneath the runways or underneath the airport buildings or land. They are listed below with known details.

Exeter Airport

This short tunnel on the Clyst Honiton Bypass in Devon is situated at the end of the Exeter Airport runway. It was opened in 2013 as a means of moving traffic away from the village of Clyst, about 5 miles east of Exeter. It doesn't quite go under the runway but is there to keep the road below the planes that take off and land at the nearby runway. It is approximately 90 yards/82 metres long.

The tunnel at the end of Exeter Airport runway in Devon. (Sue Banham)

The tunnel on the A23 that goes under the link from Gatwick Airport South Terminal to Gatwick Airport railway station. (Wendy Chatterton)

Gatwick Airport

There are two road tunnels in the vicinity of Gatwick Airport which are both split by a security fence, so one side of the tunnel is airside and the other is on land open to the general public. The biggest one is on the A23 London Road to the west of Gatwick Airport railway station and goes under the main South Terminal building. The second, on Northgate Road, is situated near to the North Terminal of Gatwick Airport and goes underneath a small hill as well as the inter-terminal transit.

Heathrow Airport

Heathrow Link Road Tunnel
Of the four road tunnels at Heathrow Airport the most well-known tunnel is the 'Heathrow Link Road Tunnel' or 'Heathrow Main Tunnel'. It goes south in a straight line from the Heathrow Spur roundabout on the M4/A4 interchange into Terminals 1, 2 and 3, which is the original airport terminal area. It was opened in 1957 and contains four tubes and has recently undergone a complete refurbishment to cope with new safety rules and heavier planes, which pass overhead on the runway.

Stanwell Moor Road Tunnel
This tunnel is situated on the A3044 road known as Stanwell Moor Road, which runs along the western edge of Heathrow Airport. It goes underneath the start of the M25 T5 spur as it crosses over the A3044 on its way into Terminal 5 of Heathrow Airport. It was opened in 2005 along with the new Terminal 5 as part of a new road layout in this area. It is a short tunnel of approximately 100 yards/91 metres in length with two lanes, one in either direction.

A London bus comes out of the tunnel that links Heathrow Airport with the A4 and M4 motorway. Note the airplane on the runway above the tunnel.

Leeds-Bradford Airport

The road tunnel at Leeds-Bradford Airport carries the A658, Victoria Avenue, a dual carriageway underneath the main runway and into the terminal of Leeds-Bradford airport. It is approximately 1,000 feet above sea level and as such is susceptible to snow falls in winter.

Luton Airport

The road tunnel at Luton Airport carries the A1018, Airport Approach Road underneath the taxiway and into the terminal of Luton airport. The tunnel is now a dual carriageway after being a two-lane tunnel with a spare lane to the east. It is situated north-east of the town of Luton.

Manchester Airport

There are two road tunnels in close proximity to each other that are on the A538, Wilmslow Road, that go underneath the runways of Manchester Airport to the south-west of the airport. One is known locally as the 'white tunnel', due to its portals being painted white, while the other is known as the 'grey tunnel', due to the colour of its portals. The white tunnel is approximately 400 yards/366 metres long, while the grey tunnel is 262 yards/240 metres long. They were both opened in 1984 and have pedestrian walkways on either side of the roadways.

The tunnel that goes under the runway at Leeds-Bradford Airport on a very wet day.

The road tunnel at Luton Airport before the roadway was widened to a dual carriageway.

The 'grey tunnel' at Manchester Airport on the A538 looking north. (Wendy Chatterton)

CHAPTER 4

Road Tunnels at Railway Stations

When Britain's railway lines were being built in the nineteenth century, many of the planned routes were through heavily built up areas in towns and cities throughout the country. To minimise noise and for safety reasons, several were built high above the houses on embankments and viaducts. As the lines reached the terminus station the number of tracks increased with several railway tracks running parallel with each other, which made the viaducts quite wide. So, as a result, many arches and tunnels were built underneath these vast viaducts that snaked their way through the towns and eventually into the countryside.

For example, in London, both London Bridge and Waterloo stations are reached by way of wide viaducts, which continue for several miles out of central London. The same could be said of railway lines in other towns such as Birmingham, Bristol, Leeds, Manchester and Glasgow. All of these places have tunnels under the viaducts, which run out of their mainline stations and are shown below.

Bangor

This road tunnel is found on the A4807, Caernarfon Road, to the west of Bangor station on the main road into Bangor from the west. It goes under the main London to Holyhead railway line, where there are four tracks passing above it. The line and the station were opened as the Chester & Holyhead Railway in May 1848.

Bath Spa

Found to the east of Bath Spa railway station, off Railway Place, this road tunnel is unusual in that it is actually a pair of tunnels approximately 20 yards/18 metres in length. The eastern bore is for road traffic only and is bi-directional, while the western bore has a roadway and pavement and is for one-way traffic from the south of the station. The tunnels pass right underneath the platforms of Bath Spa station. The railway line above the tunnels is the Great Western Main Line from London Paddington to Bristol Temple Meads which opened in 1840.

The pair of tunnels at Bath Spa station.

Birmingham Moor Street

Birmingham Moor Street is at the end of a long viaduct, which comes into Birmingham from the south east carrying the Chiltern Main Line from London Marylebone to Birmingham Snow Hill. There are two road tunnels in the vicinity of the station. The first is Park Street, where the tunnel goes under the central part of the platforms on Birmingham Moor Street station and is next to the large Selfridges' car park, which in turn is linked to Selfridges' main shop. It is a one-way street going from north to south. The second, Alison Street, goes under the southern end of the platforms of Birmingham Moor Street station and is by the entrance to the station car park. Birmingham Moor Street station was opened in 1909.

Birmingham Snow Hill

One station further north from Birmingham Moor Street is Birmingham Snow Hill, which has three road tunnels in its vicinity. These are all to the north of the station. They are from south to north Lionel Street, Water Street and Henrietta Street. Birmingham Snow Hill station was first opened in 1852 as a wooden structure but was reopened in 1871 as a permanent building. The lines north were quadrupled in 1912 when the station was rebuilt yet again, so it is thought the tunnels in their present form date from this time.

One of the tunnels going under Birmingham Moor Street station. This one is on Allison Street.

One of the tunnels near Birmingham Snow Hill station. This one is on Lionel Street.

Bristol Temple Meads

Either side of Bristol Temple Meads station, which has seven tracks to the east of the station and six to the west, can be found three tunnels that go under the tracks. The longest tunnel is that along Cattle Market Road on the east side of the station, which is approximately 100 yards/91 metres in length. To the west are the Gas Lane and Kingsland road tunnels which are around 50 yards/45 metres in length. Bristol Temple Meads is both the terminus of the Great Western Main Line from London Paddington and on the through route from Birmingham to the West Country and has a total of thirteen platforms. The present station building opened in 1845 and it is thought these three tunnels date from that period.

Just to the south of Bristol Temple Meads station can be found this tunnel on Cattle Market Road.

Known locally as the 'Hielanman's Umbrella', this tunnel on Argyle Street goes right under the concourse of Glasgow Central station.

Glasgow Central

Glasgow Central railway station is at the end of a viaduct that comes into the station from the south after crossing the River Clyde. As such there are several road tunnels that go underneath this viaduct. The two main ones are the ones to the north of the River Clyde. These are Argyle Street and Midland Street, which both run underneath the station itself. South of the river can be found Kingston Street and Nelson Street, which are both on the A8 and are one-way four-lane roads going east to west. Finally, there is Wallace Street, which is still under the viaduct which runs south from Glasgow Central.

Situated on the west side of Hyde North station this unusual road tunnel on Johnson Brook Road even has its own Tunnel street sign.

Hyde North

Hyde North station is on the Manchester Piccadilly to Rose Hill Marple line. The line to Hadfield and Glossop passes to the north of the station's platforms. There are four tracks here which go over the road tunnel underneath it in Johnson Brook Road. The station was opened in 1863, though the tunnel may have been in use before that when the lines were built during the 1840s. The tunnel is unusual in that it curves sharply in the middle, possibly the result of it being built in two stages. It is quite narrow with room for just one vehicle to pass through it at a time, though it is still bi-directional. It is also quite low with a clearance of just 9 feet and 9 inches.

Leeds

Leeds station is situated in the middle of a viaduct that stretches out on either side of the station. There are seventeen platforms and sixteen tracks at its widest, which means that roads passing underneath it go through as tunnels. There are three road tunnels that pass underneath the station, they are: Little Neville Street, Neville Street and Swinegate. Neville Street is the longest tunnel, going under the southern part of the station. It is approximately 100 yards/91 metres long and has three lanes. Running off it can be found Little Neville Street, which starts inside the tunnel and goes in a crescent shape back onto Neville Street. Finally, there is Swinegate to the east of Neville Street, which has two lanes and is approximately 70 yards/64 metres long.

The large tunnel on Neville Street, in Leeds, passes underneath the southern end of Leeds railway station.

The tunnel at Collingwood Street, in Bethnal Green, situated to the east of the station.

London

There are many road tunnels to be found in and around London's mainline stations. It is not just in the centre of London where you will find tunnels, though. There are also some examples further out. Here is a selection of the main tunnels and the stations they are connected with.

Bethnal Green

Situated on the mainline out of London's Liverpool Street station, Bethnal Green, is the first station trains reach before the line divides here. With six railway lines running together here, it is inevitable that some road tunnels will be found in the vicinity. In fact, there are four of note; two on either side of the station. The road tunnels in Brady Street and Hemming Street are situated to the west of the station, while those in Collingwood Street and Tapp Street are to the east. Both Brady Street and Collingwood Tunnels have very low ceilings with just 11-foot 6-inch clearance.

Charing Cross

Charing Cross station is situated on a high viaduct which goes over the River Thames on Hungerford Bridge. Most of the original tunnels under the station itself have now become part of businesses under the station. There is one, however, next to Embankment London Underground station, which is still in use. This is at the end of Villiers Street and carries Embankment Place under the station.

London Bridge

London Bridge station was originally opened in 1836 by the London & Greenwich Railway. Eventually three other railway companies started to bring their trains into London Bridge, which had at first been two separate stations. The lines arriving into the station from South East London and Kent come in on a 3-mile-long viaduct which started in New Cross. Under the viaduct are many arches which contain workshops and other businesses. There are also many road tunnels running underneath the viaduct, which is very wide here due to at least ten tracks running parallel to each other.

Going east from London Bridge station as far as Tower Bridge Road, the A100, the following streets run under the railway tracks as tunnels: Bermondsey Street, Shand Street, Barnham Street, Crucifix Lane, Whites Grounds, Brunswick Court and Roper Lane. On the

Bermondsey Street tunnel going underneath London Bridge station at an unusual angle.

other side of Tower Bridge Road more tunnels can be found at Tanner Street, Millstream Road, Gedling Place, Abbey Street, Marine Street, Spa Road, Dockley Road, Rail Sidings Road, St James's Road, Southwark Park Road and Rotherhithe New Road.

St Pancras International

When St Pancras station became the terminus for HS1, the station was completely modernised. Pancras Road, the A5202, originally passed the north end of the old St Pancras station, but when the station was rebuilt the new, longer platforms covered this road, effectively turning it into a tunnel.

Vauxhall

Vauxhall station is the first station you come to after leaving London Waterloo. There are eight platforms with eight railway tracks here, so roads going underneath form a tunnel. The main one is at South Lambeth Place.

The tunnel under Vauxhall railway station on South Lambeth Road, London.

London's Waterloo station goes over the A23, Westminster Bridge Road, in a wide tunnel.

Waterloo

London Waterloo station is not only the biggest railway station in Britain with twenty-four platforms, but also the busiest in terms of passengers using it. The station was opened in 1848 by the London & South Western Railway. It is accessed by a 2½-mile long viaduct. As there are eight railway tracks running along much of this route there are several road tunnels to be found underneath the viaduct, as well as numerous arches housing various businesses. Going south from London Waterloo station as far as Lambeth Road, the following streets run under the railway tracks as tunnels: Station Approach Road, Westminster Bridge Road, Upper Marsh, Carlisle Lane (first part), Centaur Street, Virgil Street and Carlisle Lane (second part).

Manchester Piccadilly

Manchester Piccadilly station, originally called Manchester London Road, was built by the Manchester & Birmingham Railway and opened in 1842. Lines from London, Leeds and Sheffield all come into the station on a mile-long viaduct, which is seven tracks wide as it approaches the station. There are several road tunnels going under the tracks here as the line goes in a south-easterly direction out of the station. Store Street is the first one but doesn't actually go under the tracks as it is situated directly underneath the main entrance to the station. It is approximately 50 yards/45 metres long. Travis Street is the first tunnel under the tracks and goes in a north-easterly direction under some of the platforms of the station. It is the longest of the tunnels here and is approximately 100 yards/90 metres long. Fairfield Street, the B6469, to the south of Travis Street, is a tunnel made up of several different bridges placed together. It is about 50 yards/45 metres long. There then follows two shorter tunnels at Hoyle Street and Chapelfield Road, which connect Temperance Street with North Western Street.

Travis Street Tunnel going underneath the platforms of Manchester Piccadilly station.

A typical red brick scene from Manchester with Bury Street tunnel to the west of Manchester Victoria station.

Manchester Victoria

Manchester Victoria station was opened in 1844 by the Liverpool & Manchester and the Lancashire & Yorkshire railways. Like Manchester Piccadilly, Manchester Victoria station was built on a high viaduct. Underneath this viaduct can be found several road tunnels. The first, at Red Bank, is situated to the east of Manchester Victoria and is approximately 50 yards/45 metres in length. Going to the west side of the station is Blackfriars Road on the A6041 and running off it is Gravel Lane. Finally, there is Bury Street, which is a typical Victorian railway tunnel made up of thousands of red bricks carrying four railway tracks above it.

To the east of Newcastle Central railway station is this tunnel on Clavering Place.

Newcastle Central

Newcastle Central station was opened by the London & North Eastern Railway in 1850, being situated on the north side of the River Tyne. A viaduct was built to the east of the station to take the East Coast mainline through the eastern part of the city. It is here that two road tunnels can be found running underneath it. The first is Orchard Street, which is approximately 50 yards/45 metres long. This road is only for taxis picking up passengers at the station, but pedestrians are able to walk through it. The second tunnel, to the east, is Clavering Place which is a two-way tunnel, wide enough for cars to park down it and is again around 50 yards/45 metres in length.

Newton Abbot

To the east of Newton Abbot station, in Devon, there are four tracks coming into the station on a viaduct. A tunnel underneath this viaduct can be found on Quay Road.

Salford Crescent

The station building at Salford Crescent railway station houses the ticket office and concourse. It is built over University Road West, forming a short tunnel of approximately 30 yards/27 metres in length.

Salford Crescent station was first opened in 1987 and has a tunnel under the main station building.

Another unusual tunnel can be found by Sowerby Bridge railway station in West Yorkshire. It curves sharply inside.

Sowerby Bridge

Holmes Road Tunnel, like Hyde North station tunnel on the other side of the Pennines, is quite unusual in that it has a sharp turn in the middle. This is caused by the fact that two different bridges have been placed together when the track bed above was widened. This tunnel was featured in the final episode of series 2 of the BBC TV drama, *Happy Valley*.

Worcester Shrub Hill

Worcester Shrub Hill station is situated on a hill overlooking the town and was opened in 1865. There are two road tunnels which go underneath the railway tracks on either side of the station. The first is on the B463, Newton Road, south of the station, and is approximately 40 yards/36 metres long. It has just a single roadway which is controlled by traffic lights. The second tunnel to the north of the station is on the B4637, Tolladine Road, and is a two-way road.

York

The tunnel on Leeman Road is situated to the north of York station, which opened in 1877. Above the road are six railway tracks going north out of York station. The tunnel is approximately 50 yards/45 metres long and has a separate pedestrian tunnel next to it.

Situated to the north of York station is Leeman Road where a tunnel runs under the East Coast mainline.

CHAPTER 5

Road Tunnels at Shopping Centres

In this section are several tunnels, which are situated under shopping centres in British towns. All of them have been built at ground level and have not been dug out. Instead the shopping centre has been built over an existing road. Due to their length I would classify them as tunnels as opposed to bridges.

Aberdeen – The Trinity Centre

The tunnel is situated on Dunburn Road, the B986, which runs from the A93, Wapping Street, near the railway station, northwards out of the city centre. The Trinity Centre itself was opened in October 1984 and the tunnel provides an underground link walkway to both the bus and train stations. The tunnel's entrance on the north side is actually Union Bridge on Union Street, which was joined to the tunnel when the centre was built. The tunnel is a dual carriageway and is around 40 yards/37 metres in length.

Aylesbury – Friars Square Shopping Centre

This short tunnel goes under the Friars Square Shopping Centre via Great Western Street and incorporates a bus station and car park with various entrances and exits. It was built in 1993 when a new indoor shopping centre was built on the site of a previous open-air shopping centre. The walls of the tunnel are decorated with large modern countryside scenes. The tunnel is approximately 50 yards/ 45 metres long and has two lanes.

Birmingham – The Bullring Shopping Centre

This tunnel connects Birmingham New Street station with Birmingham Moor Street station and runs underneath part of the Bullring shopping centre along St Martin's Queensway. The

The tunnel that goes under the Bullring Shopping Centre in the centre of Birmingham.

The eastern side of the tunnel on Fairfax Street, Bristol, which goes under the Galleries Shopping Centre.

centre was built over a previous shopping centre also called the "Bull Ring", (but as two separate words) and was opened in September 2003. The distinctive shiny frontage of Selfridges store made up of 15,000 aluminium discs can be seen at the eastern entrance to the tunnel. The tunnel is around 100 yards/90 metres in length, though not all of it is covered completely.

Bristol – The Galleries Shopping Centre

The tunnel on Fairfax Street runs underneath The Galleries shopping centre in Bristol, which was opened in October 1991. It is probably the longest road tunnel underneath a shopping centre in Britain at over 500 yards/457 metres in length. It is used primarily by cars going into to the shopping centre car park as well as a service road for deliveries to the centre. There is a pavement for pedestrians in the tunnel.

The dual carriageway tunnel that goes under the Frenchgate Shopping centre in Doncaster.

Doncaster – Frenchgate Shopping Centre

The tunnel, which goes under the Frenchgate Shopping Centre in Doncaster, is on the A630, Trafford Way, right next to the railway station at its southern end. At this entrance there is a four-lane tunnel with two lanes in each direction, as well as an entrance to Doncaster bus station. The Frenchgate Shopping Centre was opened in June 2006. During its construction, part of the tunnel collapsed injuring one of the workers. The tunnel is approximately 100 yards/90 metres long.

Glasgow – Buchanan Galleries Shopping Centre

This is where Bath Street runs under the Buchanan Galleries Shopping Centre in central Glasgow. The tunnel has two lanes and goes under the southern edge of the shopping centre. It was opened in 1999 and is one of the most expensive places for renting a retail property outside London.

Inverness – Eastgate Shopping Centre

The Eastgate Shopping Centre in Inverness was originally opened in 1983, but it wasn't until 2002 that it was extended over the Milburn Road. This involved the construction of a short tunnel over the B865 Milburn Road, which carries traffic out of the centre of Inverness to the A9.

Kingston-Upon-Thames – John Lewis

This tunnel on Horse Fair, Kingston-upon-Thames, carries the A308 from the town centre over Kingston Bridge and into Hampton Court Park. The tunnel runs underneath one of the biggest department stores in Britain, namely the John Lewis department store, which

The eastern side of the tunnel that goes under the Buchanan Galleries Shopping Centre in Glasgow. (Allan Heron)

Kingston-upon-Thames, Surrey, showing the tunnel on Horse Fair which goes under the John Lewis department store.

opened in September 1990. Its construction also involved the rerouting of Kingston's one-way system, hence the building of the tunnel underneath it. The tunnel was used as part of the route of the 2012 Olympics Men's and Women's Cycling Road Races.

Stirling – The Thistles Shopping Centre

The Thistles Shopping Centre was originally opened in 1977, but it wasn't until it was redeveloped in 1997 that three short road tunnels were built underneath it. The B8052 passes underneath the centre and connects with two short tunnels, one of which connects with the A9.

CHAPTER 6

Other Road Tunnels

In this section you will find a group of other tunnels which do not quite fit into the other categories, and which are largely unknown to the general public, apart from the locals which regularly use them. If they have a designated name at all, it is usually that of the road which goes through them.

Attadale, North West Scotland

Situated between the side of a mountain and the sea, this unusual tunnel is not strictly a tunnel as one of its sides has gaps which look out onto the water. It is known locally as the Loch Carron Avalanche Shelter and carries both a roadway and a railway line through it in two separate bores. It is situated between Attadale and Ardnarff on the A890 in north-west Scotland. It was built in the early 1970s after rocks came down the mountainside in November 1969 and blocked both the road and railway line for several months. The bore next to the mountain carries the A890 road and the bore next to Loch Carron carries the Inverness to Kyle of Lochalsh single track railway line. It is about 30 yards/27 metres in length.

Bath, Somerset

Hidden just to the east of the famous Pulteney Bridge in central Bath is this narrow tunnel on Spring Gardens Road. This road passes under the buildings on either side of Argyle Street and the street itself, which goes onto Pulteney Bridge.

Beaminster, Dorset

The Horn Hill Tunnel (or Beaminster Tunnel as it is usually called), is found to the north of the village of Beaminster on the A3066 in Dorset, which links Bridport to the south of the tunnel with Crewkerne and Yeovil to the north. It is possibly the oldest road tunnel

One of the oldest road tunnels still in use today – the Beaminster or Horn Hill Tunnel, on the A3066 in Dorset.

still open to traffic today and this can be seen in its "horseshoe" design inside, with a high roof and a narrow carriageway. It was first opened in 1832 as an easier route avoiding the steep Horn Hill, which gives the tunnel its other name. There was a toll road under Horn Hill until 1881 when the toll gates were removed. The tunnel, due to its age and extreme weather conditions, has had to be closed for repairs after several collapses. These were in 1968, 2009 and 2012; the latter leading to the deaths of two people travelling through the tunnel at the time.

Birkenhead, Wirral

In the late 1960s, when traffic congestion at the approaches to the Birkenhead side of the then Mersey Tunnel was causing major disruption in Birkenhead, the roads in this area were rerouted with new toll booths, flyovers and a tunnel. The tunnel on Chester Street was built under the approach road to the Birkenhead Tunnel and as the A41 continues it to its conclusion at Woodside, by the River Mersey, where the ferry terminal is. The tunnel was opened in 1969 and is approximately 75 yards/70 metres in length.

Blackpool, Lancashire

This unusual road tunnel can be found in the seaside resort of Blackpool in Lancashire. It was built in 1932, under the world-famous Pleasure Beach amusement park in the south of the town. Blackpool Pleasure Beach was first opened in 1896 and expanded rapidly over the next few decades into a 30-acre site. When Watson Road was built the ride The Velvet Coaster had to close. The tunnel is on Watson Road, which connects the Promenade on the seafront with Lytham Road. Nowadays the tunnel goes under part of The River Caves ride and contains the eastern entrance to the Pleasure Beach and the Arena.

The unusual tunnel at Watson Road in Blackpool which goes under the Pleasure Beach Amusement Park.

A view of two of the three road tunnels at the entrance to the Brighton Marina complex looking south.

Brighton, West Sussex

Brighton Marina, which is about 2 miles east of Brighton Pier, is connected to Marine Parade on the cliff top above it by three tunnels. These were built in the 1970s when the Marina was being constructed. The longest tunnel is on a slip road coming off the A259, Marine Drive, which goes under this road and then joins up with Marina Way, before going back under the A259 in a second tunnel and entering the Marina complex. The third tunnel is a shorter one coming out of the Marina, also on Marina Way but going north under Marine Parade They are all constructed of yellow coloured concrete. The first two of them have steep gradients, as there is a drop of around 100 feet from the main road down to the Marina.

Bristol, Avon

There are two road tunnels in Bristol which are both to the north of the city centre. The first is situated directly under the eastern end of the Clifton Suspension Bridge. This

Looking north along Portway, on the A4 in Bristol, at the 'pseudo-tunnel' situated directly underneath Brunel's Clifton Suspension Bridge.

'pseudo-tunnel' carries the A4 northwards from Bristol to Avonmouth, along the Avon Gorge. It was built in 1980 as protection from possible falling rocks above and from masonry from Brunel's famous bridge, which first opened to the public in 1864. The side facing the River Avon has concrete pillars holding up the roof and is not enclosed. The second tunnel, the Mina Road Tunnel, can be found in the St Paul's/Baptist Mills area of Bristol, just north of the city centre. It carries Mina Road north under the Bristol to Severn Beach railway line.

Cliffsend, Near Ramsgate, Kent

One of Britain's newest main road tunnels was opened in May 2012 by Norman Baker, the Local Transport Minister, as part of a major upgrade to the road system just outside the town of Ramsgate in Kent. The tunnel is known as The Cliffsend Underpass and is on Hengist Way, part of the A229, The New Kent Access Road. It goes under the village of Cliffsend, where Foades Lane and the Ramsgate to Canterbury railway line cross at the same point. The whole project took three years to complete. The tunnel is 138 yards/126 metres long and 25 metres wide and had to be box jacked into position during the summer of 2011. Six separate sections of the tunnel were cast on site and then moved into position, making this the longest jacked structure in the world.

Colwyn Bay, North Wales

This tunnel is on A55 North Wales Expressway and goes under the B5113 in Colwyn Bay, North Wales, in a dual carriageway. It also goes under Colwyn Bay railway station. The tunnel was constructed using the cut-and-cover method and was opened in 1985.

A view looking north of the recently opened Cliffsend Tunnel near Ramsgate, Kent, in 2011. (Wendy Chatterton)

An ornate tunnel complete with columns on King's Stables Road in Edinburgh.

Ecton, Staffordshire

The Swainsley Tunnel near the hamlet of Ecton, Staffordshire, in the Peak District, is a former railway tunnel. The tunnel which is 164 yards/150 metres long was originally part of the Leek & Manifold Railway. The tunnel was built as a result of Sir Thomas Wardle, a director of the railway, not wanting the view from his home, Swainsley Hall, being spoilt by the railway line! It is on a single-track road which is part of the Manifold Way.

Edinburgh, Scotland

This short tunnel is on King's Stables Road to the south of Castle Mound in Edinburgh and goes underneath Johnston Terrace, which runs downhill from the Royal Mile. It is noticeable for two obelisks at either end of it.

Glasgow, Scotland

There are two tunnels in Glasgow, both situated to the north of the city centre. The first tunnel is near Springburn and carries Darnick Street under the Glasgow Queen Street to Stepps railway line. It is a single road tunnel which is about 80 yards/73 metres in length. Due to its narrowness, traffic using the tunnel is controlled by traffic lights. Its height is 8 feet 6 inches/2.6 metres.

Further to the north in Lochburn Road, Maryhill, is this single land road tunnel which goes under the Forth & Clyde Canal. It is 9 feet 3 inches/ 2.8 metres high and is about 10 yards/9 metres in length.

A very straight and narrow tunnel on Darnick Street in Northern Glasgow. (Allan Heron)

Another narrow tunnel in Glasgow – this time hidden below a high wall of Victorian brickwork in Lochburn Road. (Allan Heron)

Possibly the lowest and shortest road tunnel in this book at Kirkintilloch, north of Glasgow.

Kirkintilloch, East Dunbartonshire

This unique road tunnel can be found on Auchendavie Road, south of the B8023, near the town of Kirkintilloch in the north-east of Glasgow. Due to its size, it could well be the shortest and smallest road tunnel in Great Britain. It is approximately 10 yards 9 metres in length and only 4 feet 9 inches/1.3 metres in height. It goes under the Forth & Clyde Canal which runs between Edinburgh and Glasgow. It is just about wide enough to take cars, but its low height stops vans and lorries passing through it. The canal was opened to traffic in 1790, but whether the tunnel was constructed at the same time is not known. If it was built then, it would predate the Reigate Tunnel by over thirty years, making it the oldest road tunnel in Great Britain.

Leeds, West Yorkshire

This short tunnel on Bridge Street goes under the Leeds Inner Ring Road in a north to south direction and is situated the north-east of Leeds city centre.

London

There are several other road tunnels and underpasses in London not already covered in this book. These five are highlighted in alphabetical order in the following sections.

Abbot Road, B125, Poplar
On the B125 Abbot Road going north is a short tunnel that goes under the A12 in Poplar, East London. It is a one-way road which meets the A12 Blackwall Tunnel Northern Approach Road at Zetland Street. It originally had two lanes in both directions, with the southbound lane being used by buses only as a contraflow, but this has been changed to one lane with a 40 mph speed limit, as the tunnel curves quite sharply to the right. It is believed the tunnel was constructed during the improvements to the A12 in the late 1980s.

A hidden tunnel on Abbot Road in London's East End that goes under the Blackwall Tunnel North Approach Road in Poplar.

Blackwall Tunnel Northern Approach Road A12, Poplar/Bow

As the A12 goes north from the Blackwall Tunnel there are two short underpasses which it passes under. The first tunnel is where the A12 passes under the A13 East India Dock Road Intersection. The second is a few miles further north from this, where the A12 goes under the A11 Bow Road at the Bow Interchange. Both tunnels are approximately 50 yards/45 metres in length and were constructed in the 1990s.

Crooked Billet Interchange, A604, Walthamstow

In the borough of Walthamstow, at the Crooked Billet Interchange on the A604 North Circular Road interchange with the B179 (Chingford Road), are two identical underpasses next to each other. They are not joined together as one long tunnel though, as there is a footbridge which goes across the North Circular Road equidistant between the two underpasses.

Westferry Circus, Canary Wharf

The most unusual 'road tunnel' of all can be found near Canary Wharf in East London. It is called 'Westferry Circus' and is a double-decked roundabout which carries the A1206 north out of the Isle of Dogs, intersecting with other minor roads. The unusual thing about its construction is that the upper level is at street level, while the lower level is completely underground. It could be argued that this lower roundabout section is effectively a tunnel, even though it is completely round. It has four entrances/exits which lead out of it.

Wick Lane, Hackney Wick

The final road tunnel in this group is the one in Hackney Wick, which goes under the A12 as Wick Lane, near to the southern edge of Victoria Park. It has a height limit of 12 feet 9 inches/3.88 metres and has traffic lights at its southern end at its junction with Monier Road.

One of two identical underpasses on the North Circular Road at the Crooked Billet Interchange in Walthamstow, East London. This is the one on the west side of the roundabout looking west.

Another unusual road tunnel. The West Ferry Circus Roundabout, near Canary Wharf, London. Traffic can go above ground or underground to make the same journey.

M1.M62, near Wakefield, West Yorkshire

Where the M1 and the M62 motorways intersect at the Lofthouse Interchange, near Wakefield in West Yorkshire, there are two short tunnels which go under these two motorways. Both tunnels are on the roadway which leaves the southbound carriageway of the M1, just before Junction 42, and joins up with the M62 westbound carriageway at Junction 29. The first tunnel goes under the M1 southbound going west to the M62. The second tunnel goes under the M62 going westbound. They are both approximately 150 yards/137 yards in length. They are known locally as the 'Lofthouse Tunnels' after the interchange which they serve.

M20/A229, near Maidstone, Kent

Just north of the Kent town of Maidstone are four parallel tunnels on the A229, which runs from Chatham to Maidstone, going under the M20 at Junction 6. They are all of the same length of about 100 yards/90 metres. Two are on the main carriageway and two are on slips roads off the A229. They were built in the 1960s when the motorway was constructed.

M20/M25, near Swanley, Kent

This short tunnel can be found where the M20 joins the M25 at Junction 3 going northwards in north-west Kent, near the town of Swanley. It is one way only for northbound traffic.

The tunnel under the M25 where the northbound carriageway of the M20 joins it. (Wendy Chatterton)

The Samphire Road Tunnel, near Dover in Kent, looking towards the main road at the top of the cliff. Note the steep gradient of the tunnel.

Samphire Hoe, near Dover, Kent

The Samphire Hoe Road Tunnel, which is situated to the south of the A20 to the west of Dover, was originally built in the 1970s during a previous attempt to build a tunnel under the English Channel. When the construction of the Channel Tunnel began in the 1990s, this area below the Shakespeare Cliffs was chosen as the best site in which to deposit the chalk spoil from the driving of the Channel Tunnel. This section of reclaimed land just below the cliffs is now a popular nature reserve, which was formally opened in 1997 as the 'Samphire Hoe Nature Reserve'. If arriving by car, as the tunnel is quite narrow, you will have to pass through a set of traffic lights for your right of way. Down at the bottom of the tunnel by the car park there is a memorial for the eleven men who lost their lives during the Channel Tunnel's construction. The site also has a lighthouse, a tea kiosk and toilets.

Portslade, West Sussex

This tunnel actually goes right underneath the A27 road by the eastern entrance to the Southwick Hill Tunnel in West Sussex. It is to the north of Portslade on Mile Oak Road, which goes north from Portslade into the South Downs, and is approximately 100 yards/90 metres in length.

Spittal, Pembrokeshire

This is another former railway tunnel which is in a remote part of south-west Wales. It is called the Spittal Road Tunnel as it is near the village of Spittal in Pembrokeshire. It goes under the London to Fishguard railway line and is about 50 yards/45 metres long. The tunnel is prone to flooding from the nearby Cleddau Wen and so there is a depth gauge by either entrance. It is also known as the Spittal Tunnel.

Another hidden tunnel unless you live in Portslade, West Sussex. This goes under the A23 trunk road right by the eastern portal of the Southwick Hill Tunnel.

CHAPTER 7

Road Tunnels Closed to the Public

There are several road tunnels which are not open to the general public, but which are still in daily or intermittent use.

Birkenhead Docks Tunnel, Merseyside

This road tunnel comes off the main Queensway or Birkenhead Tunnel between Liverpool and Birkenhead, emerging at Rendel Street in Birkenhead. It was used as a spur tunnel to Birkenhead Docks and Wallasey until 1966 when it was closed to road traffic due to the congestion it was causing – there used to be traffic lights at the junction. However, while it is closed to members of the public it is still used as a location for film shoots and for emergency practice drills.

The gates to the closed Birkenhead branch of the Queensway Tunnel in Birkenhead.

Channel Tunnel, Folkestone, Kent

while the Channel Tunnel between England and France is essentially a railway tunnel, there is a road tunnel between the two railway tunnels. This serves as an emergency escape route and as a route for service vehicles to travel to various points within the tunnel. However, the service tunnel has been used for charity events on two occasions. In 2009 former British racing driver John Surtees became the first person to drive a car through the tunnel. It was in an electric car and he had to travel at no more than 30 mph. Then, in 2018, several teenagers rode through the service tunnel in a rickshaw as part of BBC's *Children in Need* 'Rickshaw Challenge'.

Edinburgh Castle, Scotland

Built in 1990, this access tunnel was dug out of the rock from the north side of the esplanade into the castle, emerging in the Middle Ward of the castle. It is used by service vehicles going into the castle and is approximately 196 yards/180 metres long.

Gatwick Airport Tunnels

There are two road tunnels at Gatwick Airport which are 'airside' and so are only open to airport staff that have the necessary security clearance. They are both next to the tunnels at Northgate Road and on the A21 by Gatwick Airport railway station, which are open to the public, but which are divided by security fencing.

Heathrow Airside Road Tunnel, Heathrow Airport

The Heathrow Airside Road Tunnel (ART) is used to connect Terminals 1, 2 and 3 with Terminal 5 and was first opened to traffic in March 2005. It is 0.88 miles/1.42 km long with two separate tunnels next to each other. Each bore is 27 feet/8.1 metres wide.

Heathrow Cargo Road Tunnel, Heathrow Airport

This tunnel was built to connect Terminals 1, 2 and 3 to the Heathrow Cargo Terminal and to the south side of the airport. As it is airside, only personnel with security clearance may use it. It is used mainly by vehicles carrying cargo, but, since 1986, when Terminal 4 was built next to the Cargo terminal, passengers have also been able to use the tunnel. The tunnel has two lanes which are bi-directional. Each lane is 12-foot/3.7 metres wide and there is a clearance height of 16-foot 6 inches/5.03 metres. The tunnel was constructed by the boring method with cut-and-cover at either end.

The second of two road tunnels that goes under the high street in Northfleet, Kent. (Ben Warmley)

Northfleet, Kent

These two tunnels can be found in north-west Kent not far from the Ebbsfleet International railway station, near Northfleet, in Kent. They are on a private road that leads from the A226 into an industrial area and go under two chalk cliffs.

Paddington Station, London

A new road tunnel off Bridge Road, to the north of Paddington railway station in London, leads down to a taxi rank near the Circle Line platforms of the station. It is for the sole use of taxis collecting and picking up passengers from the station.

Pinnock Tunnel, near Par, Cornwall

This is a former railway tunnel on the line from St Blazey to Fowey, which closed in 1968 and is now a private road that is used by a haulage firm to bring lorries loaded with China

Clay from Par to the port of Fowey in Cornwall. It is 1,173 yards/1,073 metres long and is open several times a year to the general public, who can travel through the tunnel on a land train.

St Katharine's Way, London

At St Katharine's Dock in London, just to the east of Tower Bridge, there is a short road tunnel which goes directly under the Tower Hotel. The tunnel was formed when the hotel was built over St Katharine's Way Road in 1973. As such it is a private road and only vehicles coming to the hotel may use it. The entrance for members of the public visiting St Katharine's Dock is just to the left of the tunnel entrance.

Chapter 8

Former Road Tunnels

In this section, we will be looking at tunnels that have been closed down completely, or which are still open but not as fully functioning road tunnels.

Bluewater Quarry Haulage Tunnels

This pair of 82 yard/75-metre-long tunnels were used to bring goods into and out of the huge quarry, where the Bluewater Shopping Centre was built. Once the shopping complex was completed, they were left dormant. In 2016, plans were put forward to reopen the tunnels to link the Bluewater Shopping Centre with a large housing development on the other side of the tunnels in East Quarry.

Charmouth Tunnel, Dorset

Apart from the Beaminster Tunnel, there was another road tunnel in Dorset known as the 'Charmouth Tunnel', as it was situated about 2 miles north of the village of Charmouth. Like the Beaminster Tunnel, it was also built in 1832 and until 1991 was part of the A35. When a new by-pass section of the A35 was opened, it was no longer needed and was abandoned for several years. Then, in 2004, the tunnel area was purchased by a sports company and was converted into a shooting range, which opened in 2010.

Finnieston Tunnel, Glasgow

The Finnieston Tunnel was Glasgow's first tunnel under the River Clyde and was built in the 1890s. It had two lifts contained in specially built rotundas on either side of the Clyde to transport people, horses and motor vehicles down to the underground roadway. The shafts were 79 feet/24 metres deep and contained hydraulic lifts. There was a separate

The entrance to the former Charmouth tunnel in Dorset. This is now a shooting club called 'The Tunnel'.

pedestrian tunnel next to the road tunnel and this was closed in 1980 but still remains in situ. The road tunnel was closed to traffic about the same time and in 1986 was completely filled in. The tunnel was also known as 'Harbour Tunnel'. The two rotundas are still in use today as a restaurant and as offices.

Leake Street, Waterloo Station, London

The tunnel under London's Waterloo Railway station in Leake Street is now completely closed to motor traffic, though it is still open to the public as it is used a graffiti tunnel.

Stainer Street and Weston Street Tunnels, London Bridge Station, London

These two road tunnels originally allowed road traffic to pass under the building of London Bridge railway station in London. Then, in the years 2009 to 2017, the station was completely refurbished with all the platforms being rebuilt, a new concourse being constructed, and two new entrances being added. This meant that the two tunnels were closed and rebuilt into the fabric of the station. Stainer Street is now a pedestrian walkway within the station, while Weston Street is now part of the station concourse.

Above and below: Weston Street at London Bridge station before and after the station upgrade.

Park Tunnel, Nottingham

The Park Tunnel in Nottingham is another early road tunnel and was named after the Park Estate, which was originally a private hunting park of the owner – the Duke of Newcastle. It connects the park with Derby Road, which leads to the city centre, and was opened in 1855. The tunnel is approximately 135 yards/125 metres long with a gap in the middle for ventilation and light. The original roadway is now a public footpath, with the northern entrance accessed via a car park and a flight of stairs.

The sandstone hewn tunnels at the Park in Nottingham.

The former road tunnel under the hill at Reigate in Surrey.

Reigate Tunnel, Reigate, Surrey

The Reigate Tunnel in Surrey is thought to be the oldest road tunnel in Great Britain; opening in 1823 before most of Britain's railway tunnels had been built. Reigate is situated on the southern edge of the North Downs in Surrey, and in the early 1800s was the home of John Somers Cocks, the 1st Earl Somers, who owned a large house on top of the hill which is the site of Reigate Castle. The main road to London, the A217, was to the north of it and the town centre was to the south of it, so a tunnel under the hill was seen as the best way of connecting the two without the need of having to go round the hill. The tunnel was used by both pedestrians and motor vehicles until the 1970s when the tunnel was closed to road traffic and traffic was, once again, diverted round the edge of the hill. The reason for this was that the tunnel was too narrow for the ever-increasing numbers of two-way traffic.

while motor vehicles no longer use the tunnel, it is still open for pedestrians and cyclists to use. There is even an annual beer festival held in the tunnel. Also, there are some doorways inside the tunnel which lead to the Tunnel Road Caves – a labyrinth of caves which were originally carved out to produce silver sand.

Southchurch Road Tunnel, Southend-on-Sea, Essex

This tunnel originally ran north from Southchurch Road and went under the Victoria Circus Shopping Centre. It emerged at the Victoria Circus roundabout, next to Southend Victoria railway station. In the 2000s the local council decided to do away with the roundabout and replace it with traffic lights. As a result, the northern end of the tunnel was closed off from the Victoria Avenue roundabout and the tunnel was no longer used as a through tunnel. It is still open at its southern end and is used by service vehicles delivering goods to the shops in the Victoria Circus Shopping Centre.

The tunnel at Southchurch Road leading to the Victoria Shopping Circus in Southend-on-Sea, Essex. The other end of the tunnel has been sealed off.

CHAPTER 9

Future Road Tunnels

There have been many schemes over the years proposing new road tunnels that could be built in certain areas, ranging from tunnels under towns or rivers, and even under the sea in some cases. Here is a list of them with details of the ones most likely to happen.

Bean Road Tunnel, Bluewater, Kent

Plans to link the Bluewater Shopping Centre in Kent with a new housing estate called the Ebbsfleet Garden City, via a £12.2 million tunnel, were endorsed by Kent County Council in July 2019. It will go underneath the Bean Road and be a bus-only tunnel due to environmental concerns.

Birmingham Super Tunnel

In November 2014 a 'Super Tunnel' under Birmingham city centre was one of several proposals to combat the problem of traffic jams on the A38 road, which skirts the city centre. Others included joining together the St Chad's and Queensway tunnels.

Brynglas Tunnels, Newport

Due to the problems of frequent queues at the Brynglas Tunnels on the M4, to the west of Newport in South Wales, a second tunnel in this vicinty has been proposed. In 2012 the Welsh Assembly put forward the proposal of boring extra tunnels next to the existing Brynglas Tunnels as one of several options to relieve the congestion here.

Cardiff to Bristol Tunnel under the Bristol Channel

In 2015 plans were put forward for a 33-mile/53-km-long tunnel under the Bristol Channel, linking Cardiff with Bristol. The 'CarBri' tunnel as it was called had the aim of reducing travelling between the two cities to just under thirty minutes. The tunnel was going to cost approximately £24 billion pounds and would be open by 2020.

Hammersmith, West London

After the Hammersmith Flyer was closed to traffic for urgent repairs in 2011, proposals for a tunnel to replace the aging structure were put forward by a group of architects under the name of the 'West London Link'. These were shown to the public in February 2014.

Inner Orbital Tunnel, London

In May 2014 the then Mayor of London, Boris Johnson, outlined plans for a £30 billion 22-mile/35-km-long underground ring road around central London. 'The Inner Orbital Tunnel' would link up with major routes into the capital including the A1, the A2, the A4 and the A12 and would be a dual carriageway. The idea behind it was to remove much of the traffic from central London and send it underground instead.

Northern Cross City Corridor, Central London

This ambitious plan would see an 11-mile/18-km tunnel being built right under the centre of London starting at the A40 in Park Royal and ending at the A12 in Hackney. A second 15-mile/25-km tunnel to the south would later be built from the A4 in Chiswick to the A13 in Beckton.

Manchester to Sheffield Trans-Pennine Road Tunnel

There have beeen several plans for tunnels on future roads linking Manchester to Sheffield over the years. Most start at the M60 on the east side of Manchester and end at the M1 to the north of Sheffield. They all cross the Pennine Hills and, in particular, the Peak District National Park in various tunnels. The shortest has been 10 miles/16 kms in length, while the longest would be 18 miles/29 kms.

Oxford town centre bus-only tunnels

This is a plan to have buses running in tunnels underneath the city centre, which was first revealed in 2015.

Scotland to Northern Ireland

A tunnel (or a bridge) between Scotland and Ireland has been proposed on several occasions. Possible routes would be between the Mull of Kintyre and County Antrim, or between Stranraer and Larne.

Silvertown Tunnel, London

This tunnel would be sited to the east of the Greenwich Dome, in North Greenwich, and cross the Thames to the east of the Blackwall Tunnel approach road, in the south, and emerge at the Royal Docks in Silvertown on the north bank. Plans were passed for the 'Silvertown Tunnel' as it has come to be known in May 2018. It was planned to be open by 2021, but more recent estimates put it at 2024 at the earliest.

Stonehenge Tunnel, Wiltshire

This is a long-running tunnel saga with different proposals in the years 1995, 2002, 2005 and 2013. This tunnel would reroute the A303 under the World Heritage site of Stonehenge in Wiltshire with an 0.8-mile/1.3-km tunnel.

Thames Gateway Crossing – Tilbury to Gravesend

The Thames Gateway Tunnel is scheduled to go under the River Thames about 5 miles to the east of the Dartford Tunnel. It would join the M25, in Essex, to the M2 in Kent via a 3.2-mile/3.8-km tunnel, probably running between East Tilbury in Essex and Chalk in Kent. It is expected to cost at least £6 billion and will have three lanes in each direction on a new motorway and be ready by 2027.

Wales to Ireland

Tunnels or bridges joining Wales to the Irish Republic have also been proposed on many occasions. The routes could be between Holyhead and Dublin, or between Fishguard and Rosslare.

CHAPTER 10

Road Tunnel Websites

Below are some websites that give information on road tunnels or visits to them. Neither the author or publisher can be held responsible for the internal content of these websites, nor their functionality.

Mersey Tunnel Tour

This website gives details of guided tours behind the scenes of the Queensway Tunnel in Liverpool including the original control room, the ventilation fans and the tunnel itself.
www.merseytravel.gov.uk/tunnels/tunnel-tours

Pinnock Tunnel Visits

This website run by the PL24 Community Association gives information about the trips they organise by land train through the Pinnock Tunnel in Cornwall.
www.pl24community.org

Roads.org.uk

This comprehensive website has details of all aspects of the road network of Great Britain, including its road tunnels.
www.roads.org.uk

SABRE

The Society for All British and Irish Road Enthusiasts. A group of enthusiasts and professionals who discuss the topic of roads including tunnels.
www.sabre-roads.org.uk

Subterranea Britannica

The Society that looks at all aspects of man-made underground structures including tunnels, underground bunkers and mines.
www.subbrit.org.uk

The Road Tunnel Operator Association

A group which represents and promotes the interests of organisations that own and manage road tunnels in the British Isles. There is a useful section on the website with safety tips about driving through tunnels.
www.rtoa.org.uk

Tyne Tunnel

This website gives information about the history and construction of the second Tyne Tunnel.
www.newtynecrossing.info